WORK *WITH* ME
NOT *FOR* ME

Your Guide for Leadership and Team Building Skills To Generate The Exceptional Leader in You

"Endeavoring to inspire and train leaders to build great organizations and teams by developing future leaders in all walks of life."

LARRY A. BONORATO

DEDICATION

Judy Ingram Bonorato

Since 1970, Judy has been my best friend, wife, confidant, collaborator, soul-mate, cheerleader, and coach . . . a dedicated and loving wife and mother. She has been by my side as we relocated many times in Alabama, Georgia, North Carolina, South Carolina, and Tennessee. Through our many travels and opportunities, she has supported my efforts and pushed me to be more, do more, and achieve more. Although it has been difficult at times and wonderful at times, she has cheerfully stood by me, picking me up and pushing us forward. I am forever in debt to her.

Thank you, Judy, for all you have done, and for your enduring love and support. With you by my side, there is nothing we can't accomplish . . . together!

INVOCATION

May the Lord, our God, send his Holy Spirit to infuse those whom he has chosen to be leaders of others with courage, wisdom, honesty, and humility so that by accepting the responsibility of leadership they may organize, instruct, direct, and inspire others to reach their full potential. As leaders, please guide them as they assist those whom they lead to set and achieve their goals by encouraging and challenging them to use the gifts they have received from You for the benefit of themselves, their families, and those whom they serve.

Thank you for your purchase of *"WORK WITH ME NOT FOR ME."*

To show my appreciation please accept the following 3 bonuses:

1. <u>A downloadable workbook</u> to go along with this book. Using this workbook as you progress through the exercises in each chapter will keep you focused on growing your skills as a disciplined, exceptional leader. The workbook will also provide you with quick reference notes to use throughout your career.

2. <u>A meeting planner template</u> designed to aid you in producing an agenda for productive, organized meetings that you will be facilitating with your teams.

3. <u>Free access to our Larry on Learning blog</u> to receive timely information, articles, and interesting stories designed to keep you up-to-date with changes in market conditions and examples of how the principles in this book work in real-life situations.

CLICK HERE

to claim your 3 free bonuses

TABLE OF CONTENTS

INTRODUCTION

(Dateline: January 6, 1972; Tuscaloosa, Alabama)

On this cold cloudy morning, the young, newly promoted restaurant general manager arrived at 7:30 a.m. to assume responsibility. The previous GM had been arrested by the FBI and taken to prison at Fort Leavenworth six weeks earlier. The only manager in the restaurant was a full-time college student who was a part-time manager. The staff was willing but disorganized and untrained. The facility was not clean inside and unsightly outside. The local customers harbored a dislike for the restaurant; thus most of the clients came to the restaurant from the US highway on which the restaurant was located. To add insult to injury, they consistently ran out of the items they needed and had a warehouse full of aging stock. And, the regional manager expected a quick turnaround with no outside help.

(Dateline: March 21, 1973; Tuscaloosa, Alabama)

On this warm clear day, the same young man handed the keys to his replacement. The individual whom he had recruited and trained was ready to assume his leadership role so that the young man could take a new position as an area manager in another part of the company. The facility was gleaming inside and out, the team operated as a motivated, well-trained unit, the local population frequented the restaurant regularly, the store had just won a national sales contest, and there were 3 trained, effective leaders ready to take care of customers, team members, and the facility. That young man is writing this book today to share how you can become an effective, performance-based, and disciplined leader.

"Management is about persuading people to do things they do not want to do, while leadership is about inspiring people to do things they never thought they could."— Steve Jobs

Just like that restaurant in 1972, today many teams in business, service, sports, education, church, and government suffer from a lack of leadership. This guide will share with you how to become the exceptional, disciplined leader that you desire to be. Regardless of where you are currently in your quest to be that exceptional leader, manager, teacher, or coach, your commitment to take the necessary action to implement the winning strategies presented in this book will guide you in making decisions and building teams. Along the way, you will learn how to formulate action plans that create benchmarks to track your success.

As we progress, I must stress the need for <u>ACTION</u>. Teams and their leaders are either progressing or regressing. They never stay the same. Personnel, market conditions, new products and services, legal issues, and circumstances all change. You must commit to monitoring these changes and take advantage of them. To do nothing will lead to lackluster performance at best and abject failure at worst.

Work With Me, Not For Me is designed to challenge your beliefs about what leadership is and share how your leadership affects both you and your team. It will provide you with templates for action plans to help you use what you will learn. The techniques and strategies in this book will guide your efforts to improve your relationships with others not only in the workplace and in your professional life but also in your personal and family interactions as well. You will find many questions and exercises as you read this material. I strongly encourage you to take the time to answer the questions and do these short exercises. These actions will help you get the maximum benefit from this book.

COMMIT NOW . . .
That you will take ACTION
to improve yourself and your team.

EDUCATION WITHOUT ACTION
IS JUST ENTERTAINMENT!

SECTION ONE:

THE NEED FOR DISCIPLINED

LEADERSHIP

CHAPTER 1:
LEADERSHIP AS A DISCIPLINE

What adjectives do you associate with leadership?

- Effective
- Courageous
- Self-reliant
- Proactive
- Smart
- Strategic
- Adaptable

The standard definition of leadership is "The ability to influence, guide, and/or direct other individuals, teams, or organizations." Who is the first person you think of when you visualize a leader?

Write down their name here: ______________________________

- Is that person a good leader or a bad leader?
- How has that person affected you positively or negatively?
- Are you better because of that leader?
- What is it about that leader that you would like to learn?
- What is it about that leader that you do not want to repeat?

After you complete those questions about the leader you chose, then ask the same questions of yourself:

- Are you a good or bad leader?
- How do you affect others positively?
- How do you affect others negatively?
- Are others better because of your leadership?
- What do others want to learn from you?
- What would you like to learn to be a more dynamic and exceptional leader?

Your answers to these questions will help to guide you toward the leadership skills that you need to be successful in leading your team (or the team you want to lead). As we move ahead in our journey together, refer repeatedly back to your answers to see how the ideas and disciplines presented apply to your situation.

Because leaders serve in many different areas, their skill levels and approaches to leading may differ.

Teacher	Coach	Official
Minister	Military Officer	Owner
Manager	Director	Supervisor

Please circle the one which best describes your current position. Then put 2 circles around the position that you most want to train for. Using this exercise will help keep you focused on what you want to learn as you read this book.

My experience is that leadership is a <u>discipline</u> that centers around 5 traits that will determine whether or not you are (or will be) the leader you want to be. This model describes the traits using the acronym: TASTE:

<u>T</u>RUTH

<u>A</u>CCOUNTABILITY

<u>S</u>UPPORT

<u>T</u>RUST

<u>E</u>MPOWERMENT

Let's examine each of these traits to understand how they apply to disciplined, exceptional leadership:

TRUTH:

The duty and the responsibility of the leader is to be truthful when dealing with team members. Being deceitful or dishonest serves no useful purpose. If a team member is doing something right, let them know. If they are <u>not</u> performing correctly, let them know. Being a disciplined, responsible leader requires you to be truthful in all your interactions with team members, other team leaders, and the person you report to.

Let's look at some examples:

- You say, "You are doing great—keep up the good work."

  - If true, the team member knows you appreciate them and will continue with good performance.
  - If untrue, the team member will continue operating in a non-productive or unsafe manner. Better to have said, *"I appreciate your effort to improve. Here is a better way forward. Let me show you."*

- The team member has been warned to change their efforts to match the process that is required. They continue to not follow the process. To improve their performance you must counsel them and insist on adherence to the process:

  - If you do not address the issues with the person, they will not improve and others will see that you are not serious about the process. Be truthful to gain improvement and set the standard for performance If the issue continues, you have grounds for disciplinary action.

- As the team leader, you lie to a customer, sharing that the product will perform a certain function without getting the upgraded model.

  - You will probably lose a customer when they find out, plus their family, friends, and coworkers.

> o   Your team members will question other things that you share with them because, in your misrepresentation of the product to the customer, you have shown yourself to be an untruthful person not to be trusted.

Let me share another example of truth that shows the character of both individuals involved. The general manager tells the sales manager that he is changing the sales pay plan to save $150 per sale in commission because the percentage of commission as it relates to sales price is out of line. The GM shares that the adjustment should have no effect on the sales agents' pay and instructs the sales manager not to share the change with the sales agents. You are the sales manager. How would you handle this situation?

- Do exactly as instructed by the GM?
- Say OK to the GM, and then share the change with the agents anyway?
- Share with the GM that you can support the plan if he, the GM, makes the announcements to the agents?
- Share with the GM that your relationship with the agents is based on truth and that you cannot violate that trust?
- Resign in protest?

What would you do . . . and why? How will your decision benefit your team?

____

____

____

To say that you are committed to TRUTH is easy. It takes character and discipline to follow through. TRUTH...the 1st tenant in the TASTE model.

ACTION: Write down one or two changes that you can make in dealing with others using your renewed commitment to TRUTH. This can apply to your relationships at work, at home, or with any other group that you participate in.

1. ____

   ____

2. ____

   ____

ACCOUNTABILITY:

Out of billions of people on this planet, only 7 out of 100 can be leaders. The discipline of accountability, not just for themselves but also for their team members, sets leaders apart from those who are not. Individuals can be responsible and accountable <u>for themselves</u>. Individual accountability separates professionals from amateurs. Being accountable for <u>yourself and others</u> is required for you to become a disciplined and exceptional leader.

There are 2 parts to accountability. Let's discuss each separately.

- <u>THE LEADER'S PERSONAL ACCOUNTABILITY</u>: You must take responsibility for achieving your team's goals as well as your own goals. Let's look at some examples:

o   Your section on the assembly line is responsible for 2 functions. The 2nd team cannot start their work until the 1st team completes their work. The combined effort of this section is not producing the number of units required to meet the assembly line's quota. The 2nd team is upset with the 1st team because it feels that it cannot meet quota because the 1st team is not *"Doing its job."* When the production manager asks you why your section is not up to speed, how do you respond?

- "The 1st team is lazy; they are responsible for the slow down. I need to discuss this with the union steward."
- "The 2nd team should stop complaining and help the 1st team to prevent the slowdown and keep us on quota."
- "This is my responsibility. I will get the process ironed out to ensure that we meet our quota, so the assembly line will meet theirs."
- Your response: _______________________________
- How does your response show that you are accountable for your team's goals? ______________

   ____

o   You are a newly installed sales manager with 10 sales agents. The group has not met their quota in 4 months, which is why you were chosen to replace the previous manager. This is your first day as the leader with your new responsibilities. They are gathered together for their first sales meeting with you. How do you begin the process of improving the group so that they will meet their quota next month?

○ Your response: _______________________________

○ Your first group session with your team (whether virtually online or in-person) will either begin the process of team building or make your job much more difficult. Here is how I have approached this first group meeting opportunity.

- The first meeting is short. In it, I share that we as a team are required to produce results and that I am accountable for assisting them as individuals and as a team in achieving that goal. I let them know that I am personally responsible for helping them succeed. I ask what they expect of me and then share what I expect of them. Then I ask for suggestions on how we can improve as a team. Last, I set a time for each so we can meet one-on-one privately to discuss the way forward together.

- In our one-on-one session I will ask several questions

  - I ask again: *What do you expect of me as team leader?*

  - *What is working for you?*

  - *What is not working for you?*

- *What impediments are keeping you from meeting your goal?*
- *What training would you like to participate in to improve yourself and other team members?*
- *What can you share with others that will improve their performance?*
- *What personal goals do you have that I may help you achieve?*
- The answers to these questions will help me assist the person to set up an action plan to achieve their goals. Their achievement will help the team meet their quota and increase the team spirit for future growth.

- THE LEADER'S ACCOUNTABILITY FOR THE TEAM: Leaders are also responsible for providing assistance and guidance to help the team members achieve their individual business and personal goals. If they do not succeed, the leader does not succeed. Consider this question: If one of your team members needs to be terminated for lack of production or a violation of safety, discrimination, or company rules, who is responsible for their performance?

  o Who chose that person for that job? What vetting was done during the due diligence prior to the decision to hire them?

- o Who trained that person to do that job? Did you assign that training to another team member? Train them yourself?
- o Was the person counseled concerning very important safety rules when they started? Have they attended required safety meetings?
- o How often, if at all, did you work with that person to improve their skills so they could do their job successfully?
- o MOST IMPORTANT: You, as leader, are accountable for the success or failure of each team member.

Lastly, what responsibility do you have for the failure of this team member?

SUPPORT:

The leadership discipline of SUPPORT affects your relationships with your team members, your clients, your organization, your family, and your community. As a leader, you expect support for your decisions and the goals of your team. You also expect to have the tools and personnel to complete your tasks. Does it not stand to reason that your team members, your clients, your organization, and your family expect the same?

SUPPORT takes many forms such as:

- **Team members have the required training to do the job properly and efficiently.**

- **They have all the necessary information required to complete the job.**
- **They have the proper tools to do the job.**
- **The team is organized with the correct people assigned to the correct jobs.**
- **Good performance is recognized.**
- **Sub-par performance is addressed immediately.**
- **Team members know that they can discuss process, performance, and personal issues with you. They need to know that you will listen and if action is required that you will instigate that action. Also, if you deem that no action is required, you must communicate that as well.**
- **Substitute the phrase *"family members"* for the phrase *"team members"* and ask yourself the same questions.**

Being a good listener is imperative to being a successful leader. The old adage that God gave you two ears and one mouth so you need to listen twice as much as you talk applies if you are to be a disciplined, exceptional leader. You need to give clear detailed instructions. Then <u>follow through</u> on commitments made by you or made by individual team members. Remember; *"What you expect you must inspect."*

Let's look at this situation:

Your supervisor tells you that she has an opening in another department that she wants to fill with your best team member. Losing that team member will negatively impact the team's ability to perform their function until you can replace that person. What do you do?

- Share with your supervisor that the team member is too important to remove from your team because you cannot function effectively without her, asking her to find someone else?
- Ask for some time to get another person trained to replace her? One week? Two weeks? A month?
- Transfer her immediately and fill in yourself until you get a replacement hired or trained?
- Are there other options? ___________________________

At this point some questions come to mind:

- ***"Are you supporting your team by building your bench?"*** Sports teams must have replacements in case players get hurt, traded, or retire. What about your team? Do you have a plan in place and team members cross-trained so you can handle promotions, absences due to sickness and vacations, or those due to resignations or terminations? If you are leading a church, non-profit, or service organization, what happens when you lose an important team member due to relocation, change of interest, disagreement, or promotion? High-performance teams build their bench so they can continue to be high-performance teams!
- ***What support can you give your team to make them more productive?***

o **Training?**

- Current position refresh training—to get better at their job?
- Advanced training—to prepare them for advancement?
- Cross-training—so they can fill in as absences occur?

o **Listening?**

- What professional and personal goals do they have—so you can guide their efforts?
- Are they going through a rough time and just want someone to listen?
- Do they need to blow off some steam—better than a blowup at home or work?
- Is it possible that they have a better way for the team to be more productive? (you are NOT the ONLY source of ideas)

o **Meetings?** (We will discuss these in-depth in Chapter 20)

- Course corrections that all team members need to hear.
- Idea sessions so that all may participate.
- Share upcoming events to prepare in advance.

- Role-playing presentations so all attendees may improve their skills.

Take a moment to list some ways you can support your team or family members:

- ____
- ____
- ____
- ____

Here is a final thought on support as you build your bench by developing future leaders. The Rotary International service clubs have a process to build both leaders for their organization and leaders in their communities. They use 4 areas of service within each club: Club Service, Vocational Service, Community Service, and International Service. New members get the opportunity to choose which service area they want to participate in. Leadership training in each service area is available with progressive advancement that can lead to a Directorship. Club officers are usually chosen from this group of Directors. By using the leadership training provided in Rotary combined with the member's own initiative, Rotary grows its bench of future leaders. This allows each club to continue its success in these 4 service areas while providing its members with leadership skills they can use in their personal and professional roles.

TRUST:

Without truth, there is no trust. Integrity is built on trust, which is built on truth. Leaders need to trust their team members. Team members need to trust their leader and their other team members. How do you build trust?

- ____

- ____

- ____

Honestly presenting information, good or bad, respectfully builds trust. Every interaction you have with other people is like an emotional bank account. Good interactions, even if the information is not pleasant, build your emotional account with the other person. The more you put in, the more you have to draw on. On the other hand, every negative interaction you have with that person withdraws from the emotional bank account. Even negative information, shared respectfully, can add to the account.

Let's do an exercise:

Vanessa has been on your team for 6 months. During her tenure, she has grown in her job, and her skill level has continually improved. Her coworkers love her, and they all work together very well. Your supervisor just shared with you that another department is undergoing a restructuring and Vanessa's skills are needed on a different team. The move will result in her getting a significant pay increase. She may be unhappy with the transfer even with the pay increase and even with her understanding that her skills are needed elsewhere.

How do you share this with Vanessa? With the rest of the team?

- ____

- ____

Can you see why building an emotional bank account with your team members is so important? If they know that you are always truthful with them, they will trust you when you explain the need for Vanessa on the other team. They may not like it, but they will respect the decision because they trust you.

Now, think of a situation where you have had to present a change to your team that may not be popular. They strongly disagreed with the decision that you presented. Did you have enough in the emotional bank account for them to accept the change? How was the information received by your team?

What can you change now to start depositing into your team's emotional bank account? What would the results be if you made those changes? We can all improve. What will you commit to doing to build up the trust you have in them and the trust they have in you?

- ____

- ____

- ____

EMPOWERMENT:

Building a high-performing team is impossible without building your bench with qualified team members ready to advance whenever the need arises. Your efforts to build a qualified bench cannot occur without empowering your team members to be more, do more, and earn more. Static teams that are not empowering their members to improve will never achieve the high performance that the leader claims to want.

What is empowerment? It is the authority or the power to do something. Empowering someone creates the process of them becoming stronger and more confident—especially in controlling their life and career path. It requires that you train the person in how to do the right things as well as how to think things through before making decisions. With truth, accountability, support, and trust you will gain the confidence to empower team members to make some decisions. As they make better decisions, you can allow them to make more complicated and important decisions. This builds your bench and allows your team to advance in both skill and performance.

Let's look at 3 examples:

- Scott is a rookie quarterback who just joined your team. You have watched film and seen him in action against less experienced opponents. However, he has yet to learn your playbook and how you manage the team during games. He will most likely not be allowed to change the plays sent in to him during the game until you have confidence in his ability and you know he understands the how and why of your playbook. The longer he is with you, the more he learns. That builds your confidence in his ability so that you empower him to lead as the field general and change formations and plays as circumstances require.

- Mary is a trusted team member who just transferred into the customer service department to handle complaints and returns. Initially you allow her to make refunds up to $100 without involving a manager. As her confidence and skill in handling these issues builds, you empower her to go to $250, then to $500. Now Mary is considered to be a candidate for a management position because her skills and customer handling have increased to the point where she is ready to be trained as a manager.

- You are a church leader and need a money manager to handle the church's financial collections and obligations. Kayla, a good parishioner, works as an accounts payable clerk. You ask her to handle paying the church's bills. After 3 months of paying the bills successfully, you assign her to take over collections and bank deposits for the church. When an opening occurs at her job for someone to handle both collections as well as payables she can apply for and handle the additional responsibility because of her performance in service to the church.

In each instance, the team's performance was enhanced because you empowered team members to do more by training and supporting them. You helped them to grow personally and professionally. Take a moment to review your team members and decide how you can build a better team with a better bench of qualified candidates using the TASTE Leadership Process.

List some ways you can empower a trusted team or family member to accept more responsibility and help them use more of their God-given talents:

- ____

- ____

- ____

In Chapter 2 you will discover 4 Success Stories showing different scenarios displaying effective leadership.

CHAPTER 2:
LEADERSHIP SUCCESS STORIES

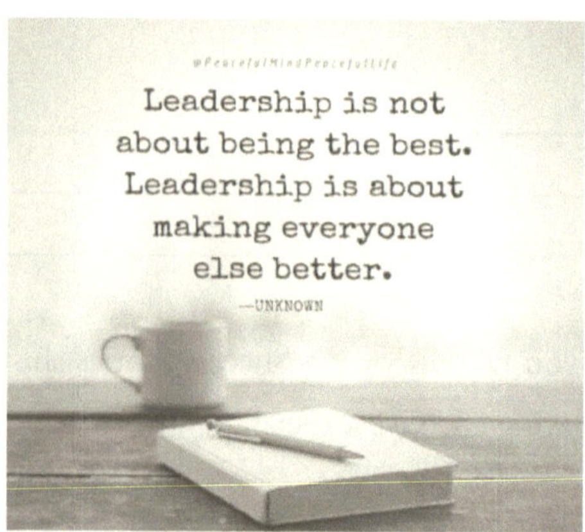

Everyone wants to win. However, very few are willing to pay the price to win. They must be led in order to do their best.

Tom Landry, Hall-of-Fame Coach of the Dallas Cowboys, was quoted once as saying that *"Coaching is the art of getting people to do what they hate to achieve what they love."*
Vince Lombardi, Hall-of-Fame Coach of the Green Bay Packers, offered this timeless quote: *"The only place success comes before work is in the dictionary."*

Both of these quotes address the need for disciplined, organized work to achieve success. As leaders, they understood that action was necessary to build winning teams. And that the action starts with the leader (the coach). That means YOU!

As he guided the NASA mission control team on the ground in Houston when the Apollo 13 space flight was in peril, Mission Control Leader Gene Kranz stated, *"Failure is not an option!"*

Are you that committed to winning?

Are you totally committed to doing what is necessary to build and maintain a winning team? Your team members will see your commitment as will your family. As the leader, your responsibility is to help those you are leading to be successful. Your success as the leader will be measured by their success.

If you are totally committed, then let's proceed.

A successful leader must master 4 areas. These are:

- PEOPLE
- PROCESSES AND SYSTEMS
- PRODUCTS AND SERVICES
- PROMOTION

We will do a deep dive into each of these in later chapters. For now, let's look at 4 real-life examples. As you are exposed to each story, notice how success was achieved or had the potential to be achieved through the execution of plans in each of these 4 areas.

#1: Transferred In to Turn Around a Challenged Organization:

An automotive group with 6 auto dealerships representing 9 automotive brands had their original General Motors dealership with Cadillac, Oldsmobile, Buick, and Chevrolet franchises that was in trouble. The store was bleeding cash, barely breaking even though sales topped $35 million. The dysfunction in the store was obvious in every department. Departments did not work with each other. The department managers did not trust each other, and there was very little positive communication or understanding of how each department's success was dependent on the success of the other departments. Adding to the misery, GM was shuttering its Oldsmobile Division in a few months, eliminating one of the 4 main sales revenue streams in this store. To get this dealership back on track, a successful manager with a positive track record (having turned around a smaller store in the group) was transferred in to lead this team. This was both a great challenge and a fantastic opportunity for me.

In the next 3 years, this dealership went from barely breaking even to turning a healthy net profit:

- Year #1: $200K net profit
- Year #2: $1.1M net profit
- Year #3: $1.7M net profit

Along the way, we closed out the Oldsmobile franchise, relocated Used Car operations to a separate facility, opened a Hyundai store, opened a Hummer store, installed a Business Development Center (BDC), added a commercial sales function, and expanded the parts sales and delivery operation.

Addressing the 4 areas required for team success made this team performance possible.

1. PEOPLE:

a. We opened the lines of communication between departments with managers learning and understanding the functions and goals of the other departments. This accomplished shared goals and outcomes and a healthy respect for the issues that the other departments dealt with.

b. We reorganized the leadership team, losing 3 managers, adding 4 managers, and getting the leaders with the right skills in charge of the departments where they would be most effective.

c. We added the accounting manager to all team leader meetings and functions. Previously accounting was excluded, creating unnecessary friction and depriving the other team leaders of needed input and information.

d. We employed an outside company to do personality evaluations for all employees and prospective new hires. This reduced turnover and assisted the team leaders in communicating better based on how team members received and processed information.

e. We committed to continuous improvement for all team members, using National Auto Dealers Association (NADA) training to increase productivity by improving skill levels.

f. The team leaders were made accountable for the performance of their team members.

g. We installed individual productivity standards for vehicle sales, service sales, parts sales, and body shop performance.

2. Processes and Systems:

a. We installed performance accountability for team leaders, requiring them to report team performances to the other team leaders. If their numbers were not in line, they were required to detail what changes they would make to meet their forecast.

b. Daily operating charts were established and to be posted by Noon the following business day, and monthly operating statements were due by the 5th working day of the next month.

c. The team leaders were required before December 15 of each year to develop their forecasts for the next year and the action plans to meet or exceed their forecasts.

d. Using NADA guides and team member interviews we adopted *"Best Practices"* as well as more effective processes so sales, service, parts, and body shop personnel would do more, be more, and earn more—making the store more profitable.

e. We examined every process and every pay plan to ensure that waste and inefficiencies were eliminated.

f. We added the BDC team to support the sales, service, and finance teams, using referrals and more effective scheduling, which created more opportunities for sales and service to increase revenue.

g. We consolidated the new and used vehicle reconditioning function into one building with dedicated service techs.

3. Products and Services:

a. We improved and enlarged our finance department operation to include an effective Helping Hand Financing (subprime) lending program.

b. We added 2 additional new car franchises: Hyundai and Hummer.

c. We added a commercial vehicle salesperson to broaden our vehicle sales and service opportunities.

d. We partnered with an outside worldwide parts company to provide Hummer parts at reduced but still profitable pricing. They also guaranteed a minimum level of parts purchases per month.

e. Using our vehicle sales forecast, we streamlined parts and vehicle inventories to have on-time availability and reduce inventory holding costs.

4. Promotion:

a. Instead of handling this function in-house, we hired a small but effective outside firm to buy our ad times. This reduced production costs and turnaround times: i.e., after the terror attacks in 2001, GM announced 0% financing on every model for 60 months. We had the plan, the spots, Point-of-Purchasing (POP) materials, etc. ready to go and on-air in 48 hours. Our competitors took 2 weeks to get going.

b. We created a yearly promotional calendar with 5 major events. Then through our marketing partner, we bought print, TV, and radio for an entire year, getting the best rates possible.

c. We put one person in charge of co-op ad funds to ensure that we took advantage of all programs, that our ads were in line with co-op requirements, and that we applied for and received all expected co-op funds.

d. We posted a monthly marketing budget for accounting, so they could issue both accurate daily operating charts and monthly operating statements, allowing us to track performance.

e. We developed and used quarterly "New Owner Clinics" to assist new vehicle owners to make better use of the features and functions of their new or used vehicle. We used these clinics to acquaint the new owners with our service personnel, collision services, our parts and accessories options, and the advantages of both maintenance and extended warranty plans.

By managing these 4 "Ps" (people, processes, products, and promotion) we were able to change paradigms and attitudes, improving both individual and team performances.

#2: Contracted to Analyze a Business by Performing Due Diligence Prior to Purchase:

An investor was looking at 3 small dealerships to purchase. He only wanted 2, so he needed both business analyses and proformas on all 3 dealerships before deciding which 2 he would purchase. I was selected for this project.

Option #1: Ford franchise in a small North Carolina town

- People:

  o The current owner had 30+ years in the local auto business and was actively involved; he also owned a farm and was a community leader who was ready to retire.

  o Qualified managers were already in place; all they needed was additional training to improve productivity.

  o The 5-person sales team (selling 40-45 units/month) was average, needing accountability and additional staffing and training.

  o The finance department was very weak, basically performing a clerical function instead of being used as a profit center.

  o The service team was average, needing additional staffing and training.

  o Parts department—there was no one really in charge and no inventory control.

  o No accountability was installed at any level in any department.

- o Most customers were farmers and small business owners with above-average credit.

- Processes:

  - o The dealership was well thought of in the community.
  - o The general sales manager had the attitude that he needed no process training and that his "non-process" was what was required to win in this town. He "knew" that his relationship with his clients was preferable to following any sales process brought in by an "outside expert."
  - o Basic sales process was not taught or learned by salespeople.
  - o No daily operating charts were issued Monday – Friday.
  - o The finance department had no accountability nor professional process, creating major legal liability and lots of lost income.
  - o Monthly operating statement were taking 15 business days to complete and publish.
  - o The customer handling process on the service drive was not taught nor being used.
  - o The parts department's lack of process created major delays in getting customer vehicles' service completed.

- Products:

  - o Vehicle inventory control needed much improvement.

- New Fords overaged with no plan to balance the inventory mix.
- Too many new Ford Cars—not enough new Ford trucks.
- Used cars: only stocking trade-ins.
- Many overaged units, some approaching 1 year in stock.
- Not purchasing vehicles needed for quick sale.

  o Parts inventory overaged.

- Too much money tied up in parts.
- Had not taken inventory in 4+ years.
- Not taking advantage of factory stocking guidelines, co-op funds, or purchase incentives.

  o Finance department needed products, processes, and accountability.

- Needed more service contract options, maintenance options, and insurance products.
- Needed product menus with all products presented to every client every time, improving profits and avoiding legal liability.
- Needed training for all products and processes.

- Promotion:

- o Need to identify target customers.
- o Need to market to prospects in neighboring small towns once people, processes, and products are in line.
- o Sell maintenance plans in finance to tie customers to the service department.
- o Produce a marketing plan and a budget to support it.
- o Make use of co-op funds in sales, service, and parts.

Forecast: With the 4 "Ps" in place and the owner taking a reasonable salary, the dealership could turn a $350K net profit per year.

Option #2: Chrysler/Dodge/Jeep/Ram franchise in a small NW Florida town

- People:

  - o Current owners had no automotive experience.
  - o Current sales manager was leaving soon; a well-qualified replacement was due in at 1st of the next month.
  - o Only 2 untrained salespeople selling 20 units/month; no sales process or computers available.
  - o One manager for both parts and service department, selling primarily warranty repair work (the least profitable and hardest to accomplish service work).
  - o Only 1 service adviser who had minimal training.
  - o Office manager was not trained in how to monitor departmental performance nor formulate an accurate

monthly statement.

- o No finance manager—thus no income from the finance department.
- o Customers were mostly low-income with substandard credit.

- Process:

  - o Processes needed to be installed in every department with training for all team members
  - o Only one PC and one Internet connection was available in the entire facility.
  - o Because having 4 brands in a small dealership requires more new vehicle inventory for each brand, the store must develop a robust dealer trade system to augment the smaller dealer inventory allowed by a limited wholesale floorplan agreement.
  - o Management staffing: only the incoming sales manager should stay; replace all other managers.
  - o Installing PCs and facility-wide Internet service would be the first step in training, monitoring, and updating systems.
  - o Develop and launch a finance department as a standalone profit center.

- Products:

- o With new systems in place:
- o The service department can sell customer-pay repair work as well as maintenance services to enhance the warranty work currently in place.
- o Parts department becomes a profit center with the changes in the service department.
- o Purchasing fast-moving, late-model used vehicles eligible for subprime financing and new enough to encourage trade-ins would positively affect used car sales and become a great source of used cars.
- o New vehicle sales increases require a shift to faster-moving SUVs and trucks and popular cars like the Charger and Challenger.
- o With the finance department, there are many opportunities to sell warranties, maintenance plans, insurance products, etc. A properly managed finance department can generate a gross profit percentage of 65% - 75%.

- • Promotion:

- o Because the local clientele was primarily subprime low-income households, local marketing should center around the availability of available credit; i.e., *"We have what you want—plus we can get you financed!"*
- o With Internet service installed in the sales department, employ web marketing to nearby Tallahassee and Lake City.

- o Ensure that co-op ad funds are identified, used for sales marketing, and collected to create the maximum exposure available for a very limited ad budget.
- o Partner with a local credit union to provide special pricing on vehicles and services for their members that will yield pre-approved clients for vehicle sales most of whom have trade-ins.

Forecast: With a large capital investment and the owner taking a minimum salary, this dealership may net only $80K - $100K per year.

OPTION #3: Chevrolet dealership in a small town in Middle Tennessee

- PEOPLE:

  - o The community has a very negative view of this dealership because of the last owner who owed everyone and left town. The original owner, a local leader who desperately wanted to sell, had repossessed the store.
  - o The sales manager, a local man, was very energetic and competent. However, he was stretched too thin concurrently acting as the sales manager, GM, and finance manager.
  - o They had only 1 salesperson and 2 techs with no service advisers or service or parts managers—hard to recruit when the store has a bad reputation in a small town.

- The office manager/controller was brand new but was highly competent and knew how to manage cash flow, monitor systems, and produce accurate daily and monthly reports.
- The only salesperson's background was in a service department, and he had difficulty selling vehicles.

- Processes:

  - The sales process was non-existent with no written sales compensation plan in place; the only salesperson was on a weekly salary.
  - The finance process was clerical only with no selling, as the store had <u>no</u> financial agreements with warranty or insurance providers and only <u>one</u> bank providing financing.
  - The service process was abbreviated, as the techs were selling service, ordering parts, and performing the work—all leading to poor productivity.
  - No process was in place for ordering or stocking parts. Techs ordered parts as needed for their repair work. The warehouse was a disorganized mess.
  - The bright spot was the new office manager/controller who displayed excellence at retrieving, processing, and reporting information as well as managing cash flow.
  - The immediate need was to recruit, hire, and train a sales team, a finance manager, and a combination manager who could handle both service and parts initially with installing a parts manager later.

- Products:

  - With only one lender available and no financial products agreement in place, the finance department was crippled. New sources of financing and an agreement for financial, warranty, and insurance products were required.

  - Due to limited available floor plan funding for new and used vehicles, they were restricted in vehicle offerings, especially in used cars. The dealership must complete a new floor plan agreement with GMAC to allow for more robust and varied new Chevrolet and used vehicle offerings. Once in place, they could purchase and display an expanded number of Chevrolet vehicles plus fast-moving, used vehicles.

  - A quick check of parts inventory showed that roughly 90% of parts in the warehouse were over a year old. The service department needed to sell off old stock and purchase fast-moving maintenance and replacement parts.

- Promotion:

  - Change the name of the dealership to denote a change in management, beginning the process of changing customer perceptions of the operation.

  - Do a visitation outreach to the local business owners to begin to repair the damaged reputation and promise better services to come soon.

- o Due to the central location of the town—close to 2 other small towns—and the same company owning the newspapers in all 3 towns, set up ads to run concurrently in all 3 newspapers, creating greater reach and getting much lower ad costs.
- o Partner with a local charity to help them raise funds and promote awareness of their goals along with current sales, service, and parts specials.
- o Offer an interview to local and surrounding media outlets.
- o Speak at local non-profit club meetings like Rotary and Lions Clubs.

Forecast: With proper management and the owner taking a small monthly salary, the dealership could produce a $150K net profit in the 1st year and a $300K net profit in the 2nd year.

RESULT: The investor and soon-to-be car dealer chose:

- Option #1 in North Carolina because of the strong and positive community standing the dealership had developed and maintained and the popularity of Ford.
- Option #3 in Tennessee because of the popularity of Chevrolet and the 2 strong managers already on board.

He rejected Option # 2 in Florida due to its isolated location, less than qualified local population, and the then lack of popularity of the brand.

Both dealerships required a lot of work on the 4 "Ps" but showed opportunity for an above-average return when the People, Processes, Products, and Promotions were improved and aligned with his financial goals.

#3: Reorganizing a Non-profit Service Organization to Meet Its Mission:

An Exchange Club on Wilmington Island (a barrier island off the coast of Savannah, GA) was struggling to attract new members even though the population of the island was growing rapidly. They needed to raise more money to support their mission of community service. Bill, the new president, a local independent CPA, set about reorganizing and reenergizing the team to accomplish their goals.

- People:

    o To make the meetings more interesting, he moved the meeting venue to a more enjoyable location. He made the caterers honorary members of the group.

    o He made the meetings more enjoyable with better food (from the new caterers) and created a more social atmosphere with a new agenda.

    o He set a goal for each member to recruit one new member and earn a dues-free membership month.

- Process:

  - He set up a schedule for each member to share his or her professional story, so they could all get to know each other better.
  - He kept the meetings exciting so members would want to participate. Different members emceed the meetings, so no one knew what to expect, making it fun and also very productive.
  - He recruited a new member who could produce a newsletter that was circulated on the island and mailed to each member.

- Product:

  - To raise the required funds, his leadership team analyzed the 2 primary fundraising events to recommend improvements or changes.

    - Savannah/Chatham County Fair: This club ran a small concession stand for the 8 days of the fair. The results had been very short of expectations for the last 3 years—only netting approximately $300 per year.
    - NIght-In-Old-Savannah Festival; The club ran a corn-on-the-cobb booth for the 3-day festival that usually netted $1200 - $1500 per year. They borrowed a 50-gallon LP gas kettle from the local Red Cross to cook the corn.

- o Because these 2 events were very labor-intensive and did not generate the income required, the leadership team held a special membership meeting to discuss changes. During this session, one of the new members noted that a local church raised $10K during a one-day sale in November every year selling fish dinners. He suggested that we use the Red Cross Kettle to make Low Country Boil dinners for the event. Another new member with a restaurant background quickly calculated that they could net $3.40 per meal by selling these at $6 apiece.

- o The decision was made to discontinue the fair fundraiser and replace it with a Low Country Boil on the 3rd Saturday in March. By having this one-day-only event, staffing was no problem and the event netted almost $5000.

- Promotion:

  - o The monthly newsletter was circulated all over the island.
  - o Flyers were placed in the windows of businesses on the island sharing news about the Low Country Boil.
  - o Auto dealers and manufacturing facilities were contacted to buy groups of dinners that volunteers would deliver.
  - o Tables and chairs were borrowed from a local church so that those who wanted to eat at the event would

have the ability. A local mortician allowed his tents to be used for the attendees. The church members sold dinners as well.

○ The local Coca-Cola bottler allowed the use of their event soda trailer. Plus, they bought dinners for their employees who were working in the plant that day.

This event was a win-win-win event for the club, the community, and for all those who donated equipment. This success was due to Bill's leadership and the group management of the 4 Ps.

#4: A Local Pastor Achieves His Mission to Serve His Parish Community and Bring More People into the Church:

Patrick, a young, Irish-born priest was filled with enthusiasm for the Lord and his congregation. The bishop had transferred him in to pastor a small church in the fishing village of Thunderbolt, GA. The Bishop knew that the population of the islands across the Wilmington River from Thunderbolt was growing rapidly. The new pastor's job would encompass strengthening the current church to serve the mainland parishioners, establishing an elementary school for current and future school children, and eventually building a new church on the largest island.

- People:

  - Current parishioners: Fr. Patrick contacted every family personally to share plans to expand church services and increase revenue to support those services. He received commitments from both families and businesses in support of the parish.

  - New parishioners: Fr. Patrick invited every new family who visited or joined the parish to come in for a personal visit and received their support of these services plus their ongoing financial commitment to fund church programs.

  - Businesses: He invited all the many businesses represented by members of the parish to provide both financial and manpower support for fundraisers such as the annual seafood dinner as well as participation in controlling the financial health of the parish. Parishioners with many different backgrounds provided the assistance required to grow the church and provide expanded services.

  - Fr. Patrick recruited and trained many more Eucharistic ministers and lectors to keep excitement for attending Mass at a very high level. These church leaders helped him extend his reach and multiply his efforts.

- Process:

  - Parishioners committed to annual giving amounts that could be paid all at once or over a period of months.

This consistent funding provided steady, consistent cash flow to fund existing programs and expand parish services. Church leaders would reach out to those who were in arrears.

- o Fr. Patrick installed a 2nd collection at the end of each Mass for the expressed purpose of updating the physical church property and building a new school.

- o By demonstrating to the bishop that the parish was wisely managing its money, the church received additional diocesan funding to be used to expand parish services and build the new school.

- o The pastor continued his commitment as the Chatham County Police chaplain. The activities and goals of the parish received wide-scale community support due to his participation with the police.

- Products:

- o Fr. Patrick reorganized the Annual Seafood Dinner as a partnership of church parishioners, contributions from local businesses, and participation from local first responders so that this event became the main fundraising event of each year.

- o Then, the parish, in conjunction with the diocese, developed, staffed, and opened a new Kindergarten – 8th-grade elementary school on Wilmington Island to serve both the families on the islands and those families on the mainland in Thunderbolt. The diocese took over the old school and orphanage complex for a new Diocesan Center.

- o A multi-purpose building was built next to the school for both church and school meetings and athletic practice and competitions.
- o The physical plant expanded to include an athletic field for football and soccer.
- o The island operations added a new parish office and a new Catholic church to serve the needs of all the parishioners living on the islands.
- o To encourage more active parishioner participation, Fr. Patrick organized the efforts of church leaders to expand the number of events held both at the church and at the school.
- o After a small fire in the choir loft at the church in Thunderbolt, Fr. Patrick used insurance proceeds, diocesan assistance, and parishioner participation to completely remodel the facility.

- • Promotion:

  - o Fr. Patrick did not use most traditional forms of marketing. Those would have been both expensive and frowned upon by the diocese.
  - o He used informal partnerships with many individuals and groups to get his message out beyond just his congregation. These included:

- City and county first responder agencies including police, paramedic, and fire departments.
- The 3 major hospitals: Memorial Medical Center, St. Joseph's Hospital, and Candler Hospital.
- Local business leaders in manufacturing, sales, retail, and transportation.
- Educators including teachers and administrators.

o He made effective use of public service announcements on local media.

Father Patrick set the standard for effective and disciplined leadership as both a pastor and a chaplain.

Leaders are needed in all facets of life: in the family, in school, in sports, in business, in government, in churches, and in service organizations.

Where are you in your current leadership role? What are you trying to accomplish?

- Have you just been hired or promoted to turn around a very challenged organization?
- Are you in a leadership position in a non-profit organization that is not meeting its service commitment or its fundraising expectations?
- Have you been transferred or promoted to a leadership position in an underperforming area of the company?

- Are you analyzing an enterprise or business opportunity and need to perform your due diligence to decide whether or not to proceed in the process?
- Are you a coach taking over an underperforming team and need to analyze the opportunity for improvement, leading to maximum performance?
- Are you a church leader who needs to better serve the congregation by increasing the reach of your church in the community?
- Or, are you a leader seeking a more effective method for forecasting goals or developing action plans to achieve those goals?

In any case, you need to develop and execute forward-thinking action plans to accomplish your team's goals. You also need a template to utilize before putting your action plans in place.

Take just a few minutes and write down what you want to accomplish and improve on by using the information and direction in this book. These goals will determine your action plans for success.

- ____
- ____
- ____
- ____

As we move forward in this examination of leadership, frequently refer back to your goals listed above. Your action plans must be aimed at achieving those goals.

In Chapter 3 we will discuss the importance of "Vision" and "Shared Vision" for those who aspire to be exceptional leaders.

CHAPTER 3: VISION

Here is one of my favorite quotes:

> *The mediocre teacher tells.*
> *The good teacher explains.*
> *The superior teacher demonstrates.*
>
> **The great teacher inspires.**
> *- William A. Ward*

INSPIRATION . . . Isn't that what a great vision creates?

A great leader is a great teacher. That leader inspires himself and others by creating a vision, communicating that vision, and surrounding himself or herself with people who share the vision, all while formulating the action plans for accomplishing that vision. Your team members, whether in a business, sports team, non-profit or service organization, church group, government agency, or political group all deserve to have the leader share the vision for the primary goal of the group.

A vision can be very simple:

- An early Microsoft vision was *"A computer on every desk in every home!"*

Or more comprehensive:

- Ford Motor Company's vision is *"People working together as a lean, global enterprise for automotive leadership…Automotive leadership is measured by the satisfaction of our customers, employees, investors, dealers, suppliers, and communities!"*
- Coca-Cola's vision is *"To craft the brands and choice of drinks that people love…to refresh them in body and spirit."*

More recently, a local Automotive Dealership BDC's vision was "To support the sales team by bringing into the showroom qualified clients to help them achieve 100 sales per month initiated through the BDC."

Let's examine some characteristics of an effective vision.

1. A vision statement describes future aspirations of an organization. It defines <u>the dream</u>, <u>the continuing goal</u>, and the <u>unconditional direction</u> that the organization is taking.
2. The vision is <u>not</u> tied to circumstances, <u>future funding,</u> <u>roadblocks,</u> or <u>obstacles</u> of any kind, nor the present availability of resources.
3. The vision <u>focuses</u> the team's or organization's sights on the <u>future</u>.

So to be clear, the vision shared by the leader with the team focuses on the continuing long-term goal(s) of the organization in such a way that each team member can visualize what that looks like. How about this:

- My vision for this book is *"Endeavoring to inspire and train leaders to build great organizations and teams by developing future leaders in all walks of life."*

  o Does this vision statement describe my aspirations for the future?
  o Does it define the continuing goal and unconditional direction for this undertaking?
  o Does it focus the reader's sights on the future of their own organization?

Here are a few more vision statements:

- Walt Disney Company's vision is *"To be one of the world's leading producers and providers of entertainment and inspiration."*
- The US Department of Agriculture's vision is *"To create a world of clean and abundant water, healthy soils, resilient landscapes, and thriving agricultural communities through voluntary conservation."*
- Rotary International's vision statement: *"Together, we see a world where people unite and take action to create lasting change – across the globe, in our communities, and in ourselves."*

Notice that each of these vision statements paints for you a mental picture of what the future should look like. Each of us sees in our own mind a picture (vision) of what the leader wants the future to look like.

The goal of creating and communicating the *"vision"* for the team or organization is to get all the team members, and even the community, to see what can be done if we focus on working together to achieve the stated goal. Because each of us envisions in our own mind what that future looks like, the vision then becomes personal to us. That is called *"SHARED VISION."*

"SHARED VISION" creates a synergy that incites the individual's desire to foster better teamwork, continuous personal and team improvement, and their own personal commitment to excellence. ALL championship teams and superior companies are committed to that *"SHARED VISION!"*

Here is a short but important exercise for you. What is your vision statement that you can simply but directly communicate to your team?

____

____

1. Does your vision statement describe the future aspirations of your organization or team?
2. Does it define the dream, the continuing goal, and the unconditional direction of the organization?
3. Does it focus your team's sights on the future?

If you cannot answer "YES" to all three of these questions about your vision statement, you need to restructure it so your vision is in alignment with the future and creates a mental picture of what your vision truly is. Last, a vision <u>not</u> shared can never become a *"SHARED VISION."*

In simple terms write down how and when you will share your vision with your team.

- ____
- ____
- ____

In Chapter 4 we will describe the differences between a leader and a manager.

CHAPTER 4: THE DIFFERENCE BETWEEN LEADERS AND MANAGERS

Early in my career as a middle manager in a corporation, I asked myself, *"How do I present policy or procedural changes to the people whom I was chosen to lead?"* It appeared that there were 2 presentation options:

1. I could present the information as a change announced by my superior. For instance, *"William, my supervisor, has changed this policy and this is how it will affect us, our operations, and you personally."*
2. Or, I could present the background information that required the change. Then, share that change without any reference to the supervisor who changed it. For instance, *"The market has changed, and our clients expect us to change the way we deliver our products to them—basically, giving our clients more options in the way they may access and use our products. Here is what we are going to do to meet this challenge, and this is how it will affect our operations and you personally."*

Option #1 is the way most middle <u>managers</u> present changes to their team. It will initiate the change and the team will follow. However, it appeared to me that using this option unnecessarily gives the team the impression that I am not in control of the change and that I am simply executing decisions made by my supervisor.

Option #2 focuses the team on <u>you as the leader</u>—not your supervisor. This displays respect for your team members and their mission and provides an avenue for them to buy into the changes required to meet the clients' expectations as opposed to simply announcing the change because William says we must do it.

Both leaders and managers are needed. <u>*Will you choose to be a Leader?*</u>

Many authors and publications interchange these nouns:

- Leader and Manager

And these verbs:

- Lead vs. Manage

Do you think that a leader and a manager are two sides of the same coin? How do you think they are different?

<u>Leader</u>:

<u>Manager</u>:

Now picture someone you think of when you envision a leader?
Then picture someone you think of when you picture a manager?
Oh! I get it:

- A leader leads.
- A manager manages.
- Is it really that simple?
- Can't a manager also be a leader?

Let's explore some areas where they differ:

VISION:

A leader inspires by sharing their vision of what the future looks like and defining what the future goals look like that will be attained regardless of obstacles or roadblocks, lack of resources, or financing. A leader sets boundaries within which the team must function in the achievement of those goals. A leader encourages creativity and originality in the pursuit of the stated goals.

Managers execute the leader's vision and plan. They work within the boundaries follow the action plans set up by the leader. Managers demand compliance in following the plan and will usually not deviate from that plan or operate outside the boundaries set by the leader.

Those 2 verbs, *inspire* and *execute,* describe the difference between leader and manager:

- **The leader *inspires* the team.**
- **The manager *executes* the plan.**

Think of it this way. In a military operation, the colonel inspires his troops/team to achieve victory over the enemy by liberating a town. The colonel puts the plan of attack and the rules of engagement together. The captains execute the plans for their companies following the plan of attack and the rules of engagement.

Question: Is it possible for a manager to also be a leader?

Using the same scenario as above, let's assume one of the companies cannot achieve its objective because the enemy is twice the expected strength in their area of operation. The captain of the pinned-down company must be assisted by the company on his left flank. The captain of the company on the left exercises some leadership, sending 2 platoons to assist the pinned-down company while using the rest of his company to drive forward to achieve their objective. Did that captain become a leader?

The answer is that different skills are required for inspiration than for execution. If a person has both skills, then, yes, the manager can also be a leader. The military trains officers to obey orders and to execute battle plans. However, they are also trained to exercise good judgment when appropriate to achieve the goal. That being said, most military officers are trained to be both.

Let's use an insurance or real estate team as an example. The general manager or broker (leader) sets the process to be used in selling, and the sales managers are required to execute the sales process in place. When the sales agent deviates from the process, the agent knows that he or she is non-compliant and will have an issue with the sales manager who requires all selling based on the stated sales process. Using this example, the general manager is the leader who formulates the sales process while the sales manager requires the agents to use it because it creates success. The sales manager is the manager who executed the plan and requires compliance.

Here is another example. In a non-profit organization, the president (leader) shares his vision for the coming year with the directors. Each of the directors is responsible for their specific area such as:

1. Meetings and guest speakers
2. Fundraising
    a. Golf tournament
    b. Silent auction
3. Educational service
    a. Local high school
    b. Local tech school
    c. Member leadership training
4. International service
    a. Sponsorship of an international exchange student
    b. Support of clean water in a Central American country
5. Governmental service
    a. Legislative lobbying
    b. Outreach to government leaders to speak at meetings

These 5 directors and the president-elect for next year work with the president to put action plans in place to accomplish their goals for the year. Each of the members has chosen which service group they will work on. These members execute the plans set by their directors. In this case, the president is the leader, and the directors are both leaders and managers.

In conclusion...

- Leaders inspire, set goals, and formulate the plan for success.
- Managers execute the plan and operate within the guidelines set by the leader.

In Section 2 we will discuss all the steps to effective forecasting.

SECTION TWO:

FORECASTING AND

BENCHMARKING

CHAPTER 5: THE NEED FOR FORECASTING AND BENCHMARKING

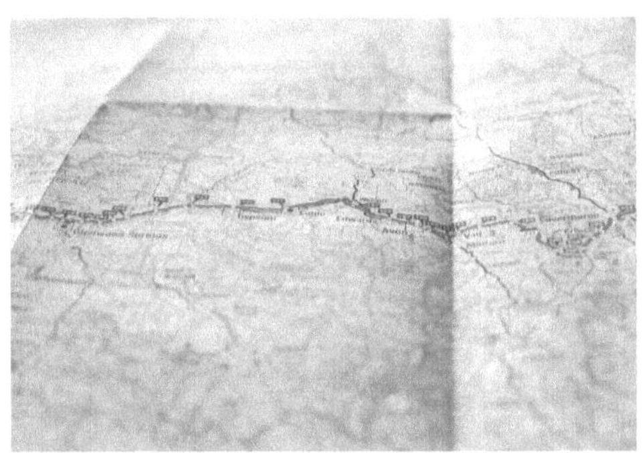

Where are you?

You are 5 days into a 15-day trip across the USA. You started in Baltimore and are traveling to Seattle. You exit your lodging and look around. Nothing looks familiar. You see no landmarks or signs. Searching for your map, you cannot find it. You have no signal on your cell phone, so the Google location map is useless. You know you need help, but you do not know anyone in this unfamiliar place. How did you get here? What do you need to do next?

In your quest to reach your goals, you get temporarily stumped. We have all been there. You know where you started. You know where you want to go. But the plan for getting to your goal seems unattainable. Team member issues, unexpected obstacles, or lack of direction have bogged you down. What do you rely on to get back on track? Two of the best tools in your arsenal to achieve your goals are forecasting and benchmarking. And those tools are used to develop action plans to achieve your goals.

Forecasting is a technique that uses historical data as inputs to make informed decisions that are predictive in determining the direction of future performance. In business, using well-researched data in a forecast allows you to predict revenues and expenses over a certain period of time such as a month, quarter, or a year. You can do the same for a service organization, church, social club, association, etc. Having a forecast gives you a goal for all the items in your forecast for that period of time. In other words, using your forecast, you know where you are and where you want to go.

Benchmarking is the process of measuring income and expenses, products and services, or performance standards against the team's previous performance or those of organizations or teams known to be leaders in similar operations.

Here are some examples:

- The best team in your area in basketball achieves the following benchmarks:

  - Averages 92 points per game
  - 89% successful in free throws
  - Only 2 unforced turnovers per game
  - Shoots 74% from the court
  - Scores 32% of their points in the lane/paint—29 points per game

- o Achieves 12 steals per game
- o Scores 13% of points on fast breaks—12 points per game
- o Is 7 of 12 in three-point goals per game—58%

- The best business in your category achieves the following benchmarks:

  - o $100,000 income per month from all sources
  - o $12,000 cost of materials per month (12%)
  - o $22,000 in labor expense per month (22%)
  - o $28,000 in fixed expense per month (28%)
  - o $9,000 in variable expense per month (9%)
  - o $71,000 total expense per month
  - o $29,000 in net profit per month

- Your best ever fundraiser for your club or organization is your annual golf tournament with the following benchmarks:

  - o 72 foursomes—288 players
  - o Total revenue = $49,800

    - $600 per foursome = $43,200
    - 27-hole sponsorships at $200 = $5400
    - Donations in lieu of sponsorships = $1200

  - o Total expenses = $19,100

- Golf course fees = $14,000
- Lunches = $2600
- Prizes = $2500

  ○ Net tournament income = $30,700

Benchmarking the best performances of similar organizations, your team, or your group gives you an idea of what is possible. Forecasting has you put in writing what is expected. Action plans describe how you plan to achieve your forecast. Here is the process.

1. Benchmark the best performers/teams so you know what the gold standard looks like.
2. Forecast so your team knows what is expected of them.
3. Develop action plans to achieve your forecast numbers.

To assist many businesses, there are industry and trade associations such as The National Restaurant Association (NRA) and the National Auto Dealers Association (NADA). Guidelines for national or international service organizations like Rotary, Exchange, Lions, and Jaycees are available as well. These groups provide their members with timely data concerning benchmarks and best practices from similar businesses, organizations, or industries located in a geographical area. For instance, NADA continues to serve its members with its *"20 Group"* program. Dealers join the program and are matched with 20 similar size dealers from different areas of the country. Participating dealers send in their monthly data and the coordinator compiles all their figures into reports ranking the dealers in various areas of dealership operations. These rankings are from best to worst in numerous categories. In addition, they receive benchmarks showing the averages of the top 10% performers and the average of all the dealers in the group. This is incredibly helpful so that all the participants can see and discuss what is being done to achieve top 10% status.

Examining this more closely, we can look at a category such as used vehicle sales compensation. If the benchmark for <u>the top 10% is 18.8%</u>, the benchmark for the <u>average dealer in the group is 20.1%,</u> and <u>your store is at 23.5%</u> then you know that you have some work to do to get that expense in line. You examine the expense report for used car sales compensation and find that your used vehicle sales manager paid out $4000 in $500 bonuses for selling overage cars. That information assists you in working with your manager to get this expense in line with the average benchmark.

- 18.8% benchmark for the best 10% of dealers
- 20.1% benchmark for the average dealer in the group
- 23.5% is your compensation percentage
- If you spent $30,000, at 3.4% over benchmark you over-spent by $1020
- Annualized that means you are on track to overspend by $12,240 this year

Using that data, you, with your manager can put an action plan in place to correct this out-of-control expense. Having this data monthly helps the GM and the owner keep controllable expenses in line and take advantage of actions to maximize income.

In another instance, one of the tactics I learned was to use a sweep account for available funds in our account over a certain amount. The bank *"sweeps"* any funds over that amount into an interest-paying account between 9:00 p.m. and 9:00 a.m. the following morning. Using this tactic, we were able to realize an additional $30,000 net profit most years.

Let's pause now for just a moment. The success of this program is based on setting goals. In our pursuit of setting and achieving our goals, let's examine what a goal looks like and its necessary components.

Remember the SMART attributes for effective goals. Effective goals must be published and must be:

- (S)pecific: <u>Clearly defined</u> in simple easy to understand terms.
- (M)easurable: <u>Requires numbers</u> or percentages so all know the measure of success.
- (A)ccountable: <u>Who is responsible</u> for ensuring that the goal is reached.
- (R)ealistic: <u>Achievable</u> based on the success of the action plan(s).
- (T)imely: <u>When</u> is the target date for achievement of the goal.

Let's use an example.

Your stated goal is to "increase revenues."

1) Is it specific? NO
2) Is it measurable? NO

3) Who is accountable? NO ONE
4) Is it realistic? MAYBE
5) Is it timely? NO

Let's fix this goal so that it follows the necessary SMART attributes:

1) Specific: Increase revenues by 10% over the previous period
2) Measurable: Previous revenue was $100,000; a 10% increase = $110,000
3) Accountable: The team leader is primarily responsible for this
4) Realistic: YES, based on anticipated sales of new products
5) Timely: This is a goal for next month

Restated then, the goal for next month is a 10% increase over the previous month, or $110,000, with the sales manager responsible for achieving this goal with his team.

List below some goals that you have for your next promotion, program, game, or month.

- ____
- ____
- ____

Apply the SMART attributes to the goal. If needed, change the goal to meet that standard. Does it make sense to you to use SMART to state your goals?

Now, let's discuss benchmarking and how to use that system to help your team, business, or organization improve its performance.

Benchmarking, done properly, compares your performance in certain ways:

- Your performance in the previous game, current season, versus your best game ever:

  - Previous game against the Wildcats: lost 87 – 73
  - Best game against the Wildcats: won 79 -75
  - Use the measures I mentioned earlier comparing your performance in that game vs. the game you won:
  - Points scored and % of successful free throws
  - Number of unforced errors
  - Total points scored and scoring percentage
  - Points scored in the lane/paint
  - Number of steals
  - Points scored on fast breaks
  - Points scores and % of 3-point shots attempted vs. 3-point goals

- Your business performance in the previous or average month, quarter, or year vs. the best in class for your class of business:

  - Gross income
  - Total material cost

- o   Total labor cost
- o   Total fixed cost
- o   Total variable cost
- o   Net income

- Your fundraising program:

  - o   Number of units sold
  - o   Total income
  - o   Total expense
  - o   Net revenue raised

There are unlimited measures of performance in every endeavor. You have to decide which performance units to measure and forecast. This requires that you have a system for measuring these performance units. For instance, if measuring the performance of a salesperson, you might use the following:

- Sales units
- Sales dollars
- Number of sales calls
- Number of appointments
- Number of appointments completed
- Percentage of appointments sold
- Number of units sold per order
- Average $ amount per order
- Percentage of customers with multiple sales

Many functions are measurable. You have to decide what items to forecast and what is the minimum acceptable performance. This creates the basis for your forecast and provides you a benchmark with which to measure performance. To have this data, you must have a person and/or a computer program to track it.

In business, it is helpful to have a Customer Relationship Management (CRM) program that will continually monitor individual and group activities. Your CRM program will also provide you with reports detailing the performance data you want to measure. Someone must be assigned to champion this program so that the information is collected and reported on time. That person is also responsible for manually spot-checking the information provided by the CRM tool.

Also in business, someone must be accountable for producing the reporting for the period of time that you are measuring. Usually that will include a monthly operating statement showing sales, expense, and profit or loss data. That document provides you with a performance document to compare with your forecast.

*** *** ***

Here is a short exercise:

Gather 10 – 15 items that you want to forecast such as income categories, expense categories, etc.

List them here:

- ____
- ____
- ____
- ____
- ____
- ____
- ____
- ____
- ____
- ____
- ____
- ____
- ____
- ____

We will learn how to configure a forecast in Chapter 6.

CHAPTER 6: GATHERING DATA FOR FORECASTING

To make a forecast, you need accurate data, usually from your operating statement or from a report in your CRM tool. The operating statement (sometimes called a profit or loss statement) is the best document to use for forecasting. Whatever you use, you must have accurate numbers to make a useful forecast.

To illustrate how this works, let's examine the method I have used for forecasting and benchmarking in the retail automobile business. I will simplify this to make it easier to understand.

In the dealership business, the office manager will publish a monthly operating statement detailing profit or losses. This statement details income and expenses shown by categories for the various departments and for the dealership as a whole. We use that information to compare with our forecast to see if our revenue and expenses are in line. Here is how I assist the department managers in making a forecast.

In any year, after the October statement is completed, I would meet with the department managers to review the statement. We will then map out what an average month's performance has been for that year. Because October is the 10th month of the year, this is accomplished by dividing the year-to-date (YTD) amount on the statement by 10 months or simply moving the decimal point on the YTD amount one space to the left to get an average month for that category.

- The 1st chart below shows these calculations:

  - Column 1 lists the various sales and expense accounts.
  - Column 2 is taken from the October profit and loss statement.
  - Column 3 is the number of months—10 since October is the 10th month.
  - Column 4 is the average month thru October: Column 2 divided by Column 3.
  - Column 5 is the percentage of sales for that line item; i.e., labor cost is 3.4% of sales.

- We now have what an average month for that year looks like. We know that November is usually slower than average and December is normally higher than average. Thus using 10 months to divide the YTD category yields us a fairly accurate number for an average month.

Breaking down YTD Income and Expenses showing an Average Month:		CURRENT YEAR DATA		
YTD ITEM	YTD AMOUNT	YTD Divided by # of mos	AVG MONTH	% of Sales
SALES	$25,000,000	10	$2,500,000	100.00%
COST OF SALES	-$10,500,000	10	-$1,050,000	-42.00%
GROSS PROFIT	$14,500,000	10	$1,450,000	58.00%
LABOR COST	-$845,000	10	-$84,500	-3.40%
VARIABLE EX-PENSE	-$565,000	10	-$56,500	-2.30%
FIXED EXPENSE	-$10,500,000	10	-$1,050,000	-42.00%
SUBTOTAL	$2,590,000	10	$259,000	10.40%
OTHER INCOME	$2,150	10	$215	0.00%
PROFIT OR LOSS	**$2,592,150**	**10**	**$259,215**	**10.40%**

Breaking down YTD Income and Expenses showing an Projected Month:		NEXT YEAR'S PROJEC-TION		
YTD ITEM	YTD AMOUNT	Avg month x # of months	AVG MONTH	% of Sales
SALES	$34,260,000	12	$2,855,000	100.00%
COST OF SALES	-$14,389,200	12	-$1,199,100	-42.00%
GROSS PROFIT	$19,870,800	12	$1,655,900	58.00%
LABOR COST	-$1,164,840	12	-$97,070	-3.40%
VARIABLE EX-PENSE	-$787,980	12	-$65,665	-2.30%
FIXED EX-PENSE	-$14,731,800	12	-$1,227,650	-43.00%
SUBTOTAL	$3,186,180	12	$265,515	9.30%
OTHER IN-COME	$32,580	12	$2,715	0.10%
PROFIT OR LOSS	$3,218,760	12	$268,230	9.40%

- This 2nd chart shows a forecast for the next year using the same sales and expense lines. Now based on the average month for the current year we need to project an average month for the next year. This requires a good deal of discussion and introspection. When the department managers list their projection numbers, they need to explain what factors they expect to occur to make this projection as accurate as possible. Let's take each category and make a forecast.

- Sales expected to increase by the following:

  o $2,500,000 current average month sales

  o +$300,000 new products sales

  o -$65,000 close out of old products

  o +$120,000 price increase on existing products

  o =$2,855,000 sales per month projection

- Cost of sales expected to remain at 42% of sales:

  o $2,855,000 is sales projection for next year

  o $2,855,000 x 42% = $1,199,100 cost of sales projection

- Gross profit calculation:

  o $2,855,000 - $1,199,100 = $1,655,900 gross profit projection

- Labor cost expected to continue at 3.4% of sales

  o $2,855,000 x 3.4% = $97,070 labor cost projection

- Variable expense expected to continue at 2.3% of sales

- o $2,855,000 x 2.3% = $65,655 variable expense projection

- Fixed expense to rise by 1% to 43% with rent and utility increases:

  - o $2,855,000 x 43% = $1,227,650 fixed expense projection

- Other income is expected to increase by $2500/month with building rental

  - o $215 + $2500 = $2715 other income projection

- To complete our forecast for the year, Column 4 is multiplied by Column 3; for instance, the projected monthly sales figure of $2,855,000 in Column 4 is multiplied by the number 12 in Column 3.
- $2,855,000 in monthly sales times 12 months = $34,260,000 in projected sales for the next year.

Using an EXCEL or Google Docs spreadsheet:

1. We used the October operating statement
2. Divide each YTD figure by 10 to show an average month this year
3. For next year's forecast, we use another spreadsheet
4. Multiply the average month's figures times 12 to get the total forecast for next year

That is the simple way to do a yearly or average monthly forecast. Then we used that as a benchmark to measure the performance each month of the next year. Comparing the average monthly forecast with actual performance shows what areas require some work to meet the forecasted goals.

CHAPTER 7: SETTING UP A FORECASTING SESSION

I mentioned in Chapter 2 that I had been transferred into a larger dealership that was quite dysfunctional. The TASTE model of managerial cooperation was non-existent between the departments and their leaders. To describe the best way to discuss, formulate, and execute a realistic forecast, it was incumbent on me to share with the department managers how we must strive to work together.

About 10 days before taking the reins at the new dealership, I asked the owner to announce my pending reassignment. During the next week, I called every manager for a one-on-one phone interview to discuss their view of what was happening, what they considered were the biggest problems, and what they would change to improve their departments and the dealership. Because calls were confidential, I did not disclose to any of the managers what was discussed with any other manager. They shared much, and I learned a lot by just listening to them.

Before I arrived, the managers began talking to each other, asking each other about their individual discussions with me. Their conversations ranged from *"Who does this guy think he is?"* to *"This is different, and maybe we ought to hear what he has to say."* The important issue was that they were talking <u>TO each other</u> instead of talking <u>AT each other</u>. Huge difference!

All the managers were gathered together at 10 a.m. on that 1ˢᵗ day when I shared just a few short items:

- "All of the conversations we had via phone were confidential and would continue to be kept confidential."
- "I was here to help and would keep an open mind and request that you do the same."
- "If I make a recommendation to you, I expect that you give it as much respect and consideration as you expect me to give you when you offer a recommendation."
- "However, if I tell you to do something, I expect it to be done."
- "We will be meeting by department shortly to set up a forecast and action plans to deliver on that forecast."
- "Last, if anyone thinks they are building my confidence in them by trashing my predecessor, you are mistaken. He is a good man and deserving of our respect."

This set the tone for the robust and productive discussions in the meetings that followed as we put together our forecasts and business plans. In these sessions, they needed to understand how what happened in their department affected other departments—and the dealership as a whole.

This event was shared with you to help you understand how to set up the sessions in which you will be formulating your forecast and having the teams develop the action plans to achieve them. Get the team leaders from each department together and share with them what to expect and that the outcome at the end would be a realistic forecast. With that forecast, they will be expected to work with their respective teams to formulate the action plan steps required to meet or exceed the forecast.

To assist the teams during these meetings, they would need information so they could understand the issues and move forward. I needed to commit that no information or data would be withheld from them as had been done in the past. I again reiterated to them that they would be accountable for requesting, retrieving, and using the information they needed to complete their work. Then, they were charged with rolling up their sleeves and getting to work with deadlines for completion.

Life rewards action! Actions get results!

Next, let's discuss the information you need to formulate a forecast. For your first forecast, you will probably not have an October operating statement. Then gather the last 3 months' data, so you can forecast an average month. Here is an example that we used to analyze prior to making a forecast for the used vehicle sales department

- By using the October statement, we only needed that statement. (You may have to use a different statement, or get 3 statements and average them).
- We got the sales data for the period in question for all individual salespeople. This included unit sales, gross profit, and productivity.
- We gathered all the information from the finance department and had one of those managers in the meeting. That

person was required to have finance department data that pertained to used vehicle sales as well as finance reporting by each finance manager and each salesperson.

- The office manager may sit in on these sessions or just be available by phone to share accounting info quickly.
- Last, I attended to facilitate (not lead) the discussion, guiding them toward the goal of producing the forecast. Very importantly, this had to be their forecast so they would buy into it and provide the energy and leadership required to achieve the forecast.
- After what was usually a 2- to 3-hour session, these managers had forecasted an average month that they could use to gauge their departmental performance for the next year.

Once the forecast for an average month was completed, the department managers were given 2 weeks to put together action plans with the input of the team members. They used the template of the "4 Ps" (People, Processes, Products, and Promotion) to guide them as they produced their action plans. These were given to me for review for clarification (if needed) and published. Like goals, action plans must be written to be valid. Having these action plans for all departments printed and in the hands of all team leaders created positive pressure to turn these plans into actions. And, we all know that life rewards action.

After these forecasts and action plans were written, we had a group manager meeting with the company controller and the owner where each department manager presented their forecast and answered questions. Having these goals written and presented made everyone, including me, accountable for meeting the forecasts and executing the action plans. It is one thing to have printed goals and action plans. Presenting these plans creates tremendous peer pressure to succeed. This process also helped the managers understand each other's jobs better and increase their skill levels, growing our bench with our organization growing as a result.

Here is a quick exercise:

Write down 1 goal for the next 30 days. Make sure it complies with the SMART guidelines for successful goals. Then write down the steps you will take to ensure that this goal is achieved. Post it where you will see it several times per day so it stays top of mind. Then celebrate with your team when the goal is achieved.

GOAL: ____

Action plan steps:

- People

- ○ ____
- ○ ____
- ○ ____

- Processes

  - ○ ____
  - ○ ____
  - ○ ____

- Products/Services

  - ○ ____
  - ○ ____
  - ○ ____

- Promotion

  - ○ ____
  - ○ ____
  - ○ ____

Be sure that your goal and action plan steps follow the SMART requirements:

- Specific
- Measurable

- Accountable
- Realistic
- Timely

As you review both your goal and your action plan steps, if you find that any of them do not meet the SMART standards, rework them until these are achieved.

In the next section, Chapters 8 – 11 we will discuss the 4 Leadership Disciplines required to create a winning team or organization.

SECTION THREE:

4 LEADERSHIP DISCIPLINES REQUIRED TO CREATE A WINNING TEAM

CHAPTER 8: PEOPLE

With your goals in place, it is time to put an action plan together to take advantage of the strengths of your current team leaders and members while eliminating staff deficiencies. The primary key to success in any endeavor involves the success of other people unless you are a one-person organization. Evaluate your current leaders (coaches) and staff individually for skills, personalities, and attitudes. Determine how many leaders or team members are required to achieve your team's goals? Ensure that every team member has a written job description outlining their duties and responsibilities. Each individual deserves to know how what they do affects other team members and clients, plus how what they do contributes to the overall success or failure of the organization. *"Hire for attitude...train for skills."*

To meet or exceed your forecast, you must determine the skills required to accomplish your goals. The processes you choose to achieve them will affect these skills and the number of people required to complete the numerous designated tasks. A company that delivers a product or service to its customer will differ from one whose clients all come to their location. Also, staffing for an organization that delivers products to a warehouse or wholesale seller will differ from one that delivers to the end-user.

- If providing both products and services, will those require different staffing or can the same personnel complete both tasks?
- What budget have you put in place for staffing team members and team leaders?
- Remember that investing in training should make your team members more productive, so be sure you have budgeted enough for team members professional skills improvement.

While reviewing with your teams their current performance data versus what is needed to meet the forecast, ask open-ended questions to determine the mindset of these individuals, their expectations as well as their personal goals and motivations. For example, a team member with a goal for this year of getting out of renting and buying their first home will have a different motivation than one who is saving for a vacation to Disneyland. This review will also reveal issues that may impede them in the performance of their tasks.

Does the individual have a written job description to guide them in their daily activities? If they have a skills issue, can this individual be trained to do their job properly? What training, either in-house, online, or at a remote location, will bring the skill level up to an acceptable level? How much should be budgeted for this training. If you determine that this person is not suited for their current position, would this team member achieve better performance in another role within the organization?

Utilization of a basic personality evaluation survey will help the leader understand the way team members process information and how they relate and react to other different personalities. An accurate survey determining their dominant personality type will also inform leaders on how to effectively coach them to be more productive and work better with other team members. Understand that certain personalities are better suited to certain jobs. This will allow you to put the right people in the best job for them.

For example, individuals who are very structured and detail-oriented usually do very well in clerical, accounting, and warehouse functions. Their personalities may have difficulty accepting or adjusting to major changes but allow them to function well under strict rules. Extroverted individuals with a strong desire to be seen as successful and possess above average communication skills usually do well in sales where rapid adjustment to the individual or company you are selling is a forerunner to successful selling. Team members with strong, dominant personalities thrive on change as long as it leads to their success and they have no trouble making decisions and taking responsibility for them. They are task-oriented and results-oriented, so leadership is much more comfortable for them than other personality types. This is a very basic overview of some of the major personality types. The personality evaluation system that you use will have much more detail to help you understand how the individuals you want for certain jobs will approach their work, how they communicate with others, and how best to coach them. If you have a human resources department or person, find out what tools are available for personality evaluations.

Putting the right people in the right jobs based on skills, personalities, and attitudes will be invaluable in propelling you to meet your forecast. Here are some examples:

- Willard worked in a dealership call center. He performed at an above-average level at his job, but his drive made him desire more challenge and recognition for his achievement. We transferred him to the sales floor, and he immediately used his drive and wonderful personality to exceed all expectations as a sales agent.

- Dennis was a teenager who was working part-time as an average fry cook at a restaurant. He had a very peculiar personality that attracted attention—in a good way. While competing in a nationwide dessert sales contest, his manager asked him to dress up as "Grandma Hardee" and push desserts during lunch and dinner. Diners loved him so much that 7 out of 10 bought from him, and the restaurant won the national sales contest.

- Melissa, who was working in a dealership service center, was very organized, and took on more responsibility than her clerical role required of her. Her customers loved her but, she clashed daily with her coworkers. She was transferred to their BDC, where her customer care, personal drive and accountability along with the sales training she received, pushed up the volume in the call center and doubled her income.

- Steve was a somewhat average car sales agent struggling to succeed. He did not do well with the structure and control of the system that he worked under. To succeed, he left the dealership, earned his real estate license, and tripled his income selling houses where strict structure did not impede his creativity but allowed him to blossom in a more open environment.

These are just a few of the thousands of examples of putting the right people in the right jobs where their personalities, skills, and attitudes improved sales and customer service. These transfers also provided them with more personal satisfaction while helping them earn more money. That is a win-win-win for themselves, co-workers, customers, and the organizations.

For those who do not measure up, you must decide to retrain them, put them in positions where their skills will allow them to succeed, or terminate them. This sounds harsh, but keeping people in positions where they cannot perform hurts the individual, your clients, the team, and ultimately your organization or business. Look at the examples listed above. Steve ultimately achieved his version of success by leaving and seeking another career. Melissa and Willard were transferred into new positions at the same business and achieved success. Dennis was retrained to be a better fry cook, and his level of confidence was raised significantly with his "Grandma Hardee" stint. Which is more humane, keeping a person in a job where they cannot excel, or allowing them to grow and prosper either with your team or someone else's team?

Do you have an individual on your team that is not performing up to their potential? Honestly answer the question, "why?" List that person and share what you can do to help that individual succeed:

NAME: ____

Your plan: _______________________________________

____

In the 1950s and into the 1970s, a college football coach recruited players based on speed and athletic ability at a time when most college coaches wanted bigger, brawnier players. He wanted more speed so that his offensive and defensive plays would develop before their opponents could react. He wanted more athletic players so that they could outlast their opponents through the 4th quarter. His staunch determination to win and his consistently strong emphasis on discipline created successful teams that for a generation were the standards against which all other college football teams would be compared. He achieved a .780 total winning record, took 29 teams to bowl games, and won 15 conference championships and 6 national championships. His success was achieved by knowing what skills were required at each position, putting the right people, both coaches and players, in the best positions for their skills, and maintaining an unshakable determination for everyone in the program to perform at their best. He was also the first to congratulate others whenever the team won and take personal responsibility whenever they lost. This leader was Paul "Bear" Bryant.

Do you need new team members to achieve your goals? How many new team members are required to achieve your team's goals? How will you attract, hire, train, motivate, organize, and retain team members? Who will be accountable for these functions? How will your people be compensated?

- Hourly? Using a written timesheet, a computer log, a time clock?
- Salary only? Per week, per month?
- Salary plus bonus?
- Salary plus commission?
- Commission paid weekly?
- Commission paid monthly with a weekly draw?

Each method of compensation has its advantages and disadvantages. What is critically important is that you are consistent and that compensation changes are <u>rare</u> and only adjusted when <u>absolutely necessary</u>. Since most people live from paycheck to paycheck, changes in compensation can demoralize people quickly. If you must make a change, be sure to explain it honestly and show your people how they can take advantage of the change.

Let me state again that your team members must have written job descriptions with individual and team goals so they know how they will be measured. This applies to team leaders as well as team members. As you review these descriptions with your staff members, be prepared to update these descriptions to meet changing needs or new processes. Schedule training for those who need help in improving their skills. Getting input from individual team members will allow them to "buy-in" to the team's goals. Plus it aids them in better understanding their role in achieving those goals and allows you better insight into how the team member will best contribute to the success of the team.

This bears repeating: as you put your team together be sure to

<u>"Hire for Attitude—Train for Skills."</u>

Attitudes cannot be taught. Conversely, an individual with a servant attitude who wants to excel in their job and help the team can learn skills. Substandard performance cannot be tolerated. Above-average performance must be congratulated and rewarded. Remember, choices you make regarding the people on your team will, to a great degree, determine your success. That is why the PEOPLE segment of your action plan requires the most time to formulate and will be the primary reason for the success or failure of your organization.

Finally, in our discussion of people requirements, we must reiterate the importance of staff and leadership continuous training. This includes everyone in the organization from leadership, accounting, production, sales, service, etc. Winning organizations (teams) commit to continuous improvement that can only be achieved by having a training schedule set in place for everyone, including the leader. Leaders set the example by participating in their own self-improvement and by having a member of the leadership team contribute during training sessions for team members. Inasmuch as everyone benefits personally from scheduled training, your organization will reap the rewards of improved morale, better customer service, and increased productivity.

CHAPTER 9:
PROCESSES AND SYSTEMS

Having great people using non-productive processes will not produce success. Every endeavor has its *best practices,* and those practices change and get better as challenges and opportunities occur. For instance, the Internet, email, texting, social media, and numerous other factors have changed what we sell and service and how we bring those products and services to market. Did COVID-19 affect how and what you bought or where you bought it? Did it affect how and when you traveled? The marketplace changed, allowing clients to stay safe and still get what they wanted and needed. Streamline your processes to best serve your clients.

Be sure to have your processes written and communicated to your team members. Train your team members so they understand why these processes are important to the overall success of the team. Have your team leaders ensure the consistent performance of these processes. However, be prepared to augment, update, or change non-productive processes as circumstances make old processes obsolete. Let's examine some examples:

- A head football coach religiously reviews game films of their most recent game and films of their next opponent with his assistant coaches and players. The data from the films are used to improve both individual and team performances and to create a game plan, making adjustments for their next opponent.

- In a restaurant where different diners at the same table order different menu items requiring different cook times and equipment, i.e., pan-seared fish, grilled steak, shrimp scampi, and fried chicken, there must be a process in place to ensure that these 4 dishes are ready at the same time, so the diners will be served their orders at the correct temperature for each dish and at the same time for them to enjoy their dining experience.

- On a factory assembly line where a complex device is being manufactured, a team of 6 workers at workstation 18A must use the best process, ensuring their portion of the assembly is completed on time. For instance, one will bring the parts to the line, two will complete one section, two will complete the next section, and one will assist where needed.

- When a non-profit group runs an annual golf tournament to raise funds for charity, the chairperson reviews the previous year's event with his team. They commit to processes in place and make adjustments to ensure that all foursomes are filled. There must be processes in place before, during, and after the tournament to handle the event and achieve the fundraising goal. The team knows that this year's smooth performance and how well the participants in this golf tournament enjoy the outing affects the success of next year's event.

All these examples and many more provide proof that the best processes performed by well-trained and accountable team members achieve the best results. Is there any doubt that teams coached by Pat Riley both in Los Angeles and Miami or teams coached by John Wooden at UCLA outperformed most other basketball teams consistently because of the great processes they use before, during, and after games, putting them in the best position to win?

Just like goals that are not written are only wishes, processes that are not written nor enforced are only myths. Recently after a ball game for my grandson, my wife and I went through the drive-through at a local fast-food chicken restaurant. The team member taking the order was pleasant and answered our questions. When we drove up to the drive-thru window the team member paid us no attention for a full minute, as he was showing off his dance moves to his coworkers. He was pleasant and let us know that it would be just a few more moments for our order to be ready. He wanted to wait to take our money until the order was ready. I suggested it may be best if we paid while we were waiting. When the order was ready, he put the food haphazardly in the bag and it spilled out. He also did not check to see if there was sauce—there was not. Having worked for 12 years in the restaurant business, I must conclude that somewhere in the franchise documents exist written processes for customer interactions, assembling to-go orders, taking the customer's money, and verifying that the order is correct. Even a written process is of no use if the team members empowered to perform the process and the team leader responsible for ensuring that the process is followed do not follow that process.

Let's use the restaurant as an example of the process:

- The process of taking, handling, and delivering the take-out window order to the customer.

   1. With the customer at the microphone, the order taker greets the customer, answers any questions, takes the order, enters it into the system, repeats the order to ensure its accuracy, shares the total price, and instructs the customer to drive around.

   2. As soon as the order is input, the kitchen personnel see the order and begin the process of cooking and assembling the order. The assembler puts the order together for delivery to the 2nd window. Kitchen staff begins special orders.

   3. When the customer reaches the 1st window, the order taker repeats the order to ensure the order has been put in correctly. They complete the monetary transaction and instruct the customer to proceed to the next window.

   4. The assembler is responsible for proper packaging of

the order, its delivery to window #2, and the accuracy of the order.

5. The window person at window #2 draws the drinks and prepares them for handoff to the customer. They are also responsible for checking the order to ensure accuracy.

6. When the customer arrives at window #2, the window person repeats the order back to the customer. If there are issues, the process stops, and the window person and the assembler address the problem and get it corrected.

7. The window person delivers the assembled order to the customer along with any requests for extra napkins, condiments, etc. Then the customer is thanked warmly and invited to return again soon!

8. Time to order and transaction complete with the customer leaving the 2nd window is 1 – 3 minutes depending on traffic volume.

Notice that this process is specific, shows who is responsible, and provides fast efficient service, which is what customers expect from a fast-food operation.

Take just a moment now and write out one of your basic processes step-by-step.

- What outcome is expected by following this process?

o ____

- Which team members will be involved?

  - _______________________________________

- Who is responsible for this process being followed?

  - _______________________________________

- Where will this be done?

  - _______________________________________

- How long should it take to accomplish this task?

  - _______________________________________

- Why should this process be followed to complete this task?

  - _______________________________________

Great teams have great processes. This is true if you coach a sports team, run a service organization, operate a business, are building a structure, or manage an office team or a church organization. Each team member must understand the importance of following these processes to their successful conclusion.

During your interactions with team members, determine what your clients want and how you can best deliver it to them as quickly and efficiently as possible. For instance, clients using your website Q&A section ask how they can best use your product or service. They also use that section to ask why your organization does not provide what they want the way they want it. Use this same Q&A section to determine what changes the organization needs to make and what new products or services it needs to offer. Then change your processes to accommodate these new opportunities.

Here is another short story to emphasize how processes need to be changed when events or circumstances occur. Early in the Vietnam war, when a US Army platoon was moving up a trail or road and they were attacked from the left side of the road, they would quickly take cover on the right side of the road. The Viet Cong saw this and changed tactics by digging deep trenches on the right side of the road, filling the trenches with sharp, poisoned bamboo stakes, and then covering the pit with small branches and grass. When the soldier fell into the trench, if being impaled on the stake did not kill him, he would die slowly of severe blood poisoning. The US Army changed tactics so that when they were attacked from one side of the road, instead of retreating to the opposite side of the road, they immediately attacked the area from which the fire was coming. This change proved effective until the enemy changed tactics again.

Strategic and tactical changes are made in our military based on the information in After Action Reports. After Action Reports for the military are like game films for a sports team. In both cases, teams and their leaders analyze their actions and make the necessary changes to meet new challenges and take advantage of new opportunities. How often do you, as the leader, discuss your operations with the people who perform the tasks? When you are analyzing processes, your people can provide you with on-the-job immediate feedback. This feedback can be used to affirm the usefulness of your processes or indicate the need to update or alter them.

Advanced newer technology and obsolete technology can dictate what systems or processes need to be addressed. New Customer Relationship software programs have changed how sales organizations contact their clients, sell products and services, follow up to ensure a positive experience, and share new opportunities to serve those clients. Which of your processes need to be updated, streamlined, or changed completely, as they are keeping your team from more effectively accomplishing their objectives?

If you are leading a team in a certain industry, there may be an opportunity for you to use trade organizations and their publications or websites to view Best Practices that others in that industry have found to make them more productive. These Best Practices may create different processes, use different equipment, or take advantage of different materials. They may even show you a new product or service that you can utilize to augment what you are currently offering. These associations are great sources of information for you to keep your team more productive.

<u>Eliminate roadblocks to productivity</u>. As an example, the retail automobile business has changed so that buyers no longer have

to visit 5 dealerships for information. They can shop online, get approved online, and have the vehicle delivered to their home or work. Sellers who altered their efforts to accommodate changing customer expectations and attitudes left behind those dealership teams who did not change their processes to accommodate buyers' needs and desires.

Organizations with Great Processes get Great Results.

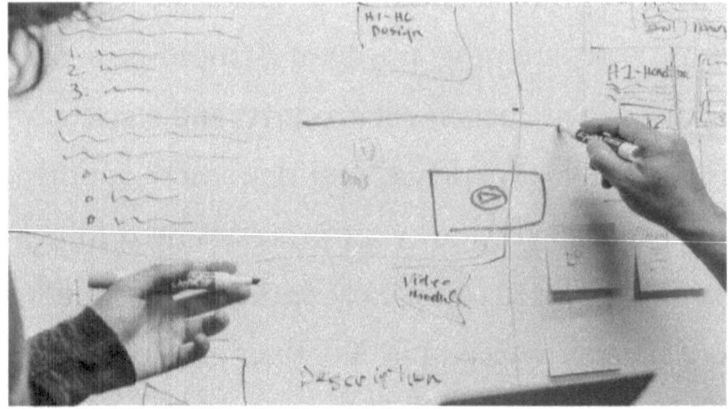

In Chapter 10, we will discuss Products and Services in our journey to develop our effective action plans.

CHAPTER 10:
PRODUCTS AND SERVICES

What exactly is it that you are selling? Is it products or services or both? You may have fewer than five items or several thousand products. What you are selling may be tangible products like food, equipment, real estate, consumer items, raw materials for manufacturing, or building materials. Or it could be intangible products such as insurance, web, radio or TV advertising, or self-help classes. Let's examine some options starting with products. We will look at services a little later in this chapter.

PRODUCTS:

First, you need to list exactly what products or groups of products you are selling. Are you buying and reselling these products or producing them yourself? If you are producing or assembling the products to be sold, you will need to list what materials are needed for production. The more complete and accurate list of products you are selling the more equipped you will be in developing a stocking level for these products and/or the materials to make them.

Next, where will you be selling the products? In your facility? Online? Through franchised dealers or stores? If they are not being sold in your facility, how will the products be delivered to your customers? Will you use a delivery service such as USPS, UPS, or FedEx? Will they be delivered in your vehicles? Or will the customers be required to get them at your facility?

Who are your primary customers? Will they be Business to Business (B2B) or wholesale customers? Or, will they be Business to Customer (B2C) or retail customers. Where are they located? Can they be identified or segmented by gender, age, education, geography, income, or previous ownership? Where will they be buying your products, in-store, online, in person, or through a purchasing manager? Having a good grasp of who your customers are and their characteristics, along with where they will be buying, will aid you in producing a stocking level or guide.

For tangible products, you will need to build a stocking level. A stocking level will help you have products available when your customers want them while reducing the carrying costs of having too much money tied up in slow-moving inventory. A stocking level must take into account where you are selling these products, who are your primary customers, and how much lead time is required between ordering and having the products delivered to you or your customer. Will these products be ones you are making or products that you buy and resell?

Here is a basic guide to building a stocking level by hand. If you desire to have a 30-day supply of product or material, use your sales data for the last 6 months to determine the number for a 30-day supply. For instance, if you sold 150 of a certain item in the last 6 months, your 30-day supply will be 25. That is the amount of that product you should have available at any given time. Any less than that and you run the risk of not having enough product to satisfy your customers' needs. More than that amount may mean you have cash issues because you have too much money tied up in overaged inventory on your shelves or in your warehouse. Your stocking guide may vary due to special events or seasonal changes that occur every year. If Christmas or Valentine's Day double the demand for your products, then you will need to plan for the increase to ensure an adequate level of product during those selling seasons to meet the anticipated demand. This stocking level process also applies to producers that are making the products and must store the materials to produce them.

This basic guide to building a stocking level is <u>not</u> recommending a 30-day supply of products or materials. You must decide on the day's supply that is best for your firm and then manage it based on events that affect your business. If you have a supplier who delivers products to you 3 times per week you may decide that a 10- or 15-day supply is best and order accordingly. On the other hand, if your sales vary widely from week to week or month to month, you may decide that a 60-day or 90-day supply is better for you, especially if the products you sell come from overseas and the lead time from order to delivery is 4 months. Many software solutions to help you control your inventory stocking level are available. Most industries have groups that review and recommend software vendors to help you take and keep control of your inventories.

Here is another facet of your stocking guide to be addressed. Let's explore this with two queries.

1. What process do you use to ensure that when you order this item for your customer, they will actually buy it?
2. Also, when you do sell this item, what process do you use for putting this item into your stocking guide?

For question #1: Do you require that the item be paid for in advance? Or that they pay 50% in advance? Or, do you simply order the item and promise to contact the customer when it arrives? This is critical because many buyers will keep searching, and if they find the item before their "special order" arrives, they will buy it, and you will be stuck with a special order that is outside of your stocking guide.

For question #2: What is your process for stocking a new item that is not currently in your stocking guide? Do you order another as soon as you sell the 1st one? Do you have to sell a certain number within a specified period to add it to your stocking guide? (i.e., if you sell 3 of an item within 3 months, will you add that to your stocking guide?)

How about new products that are presented to you because your customer base represents the demographic that the vendor wants to reach? Will you stock them if the first order is on consignment, or if the vendor will not require payment for 30 – 60 days? The answers to these questions will affect your stocking guide.

For intangible products like media advertising, your only limits will be on-air time, space available, and industry, platform, or government regulations. Intangibles like insurance, online education, warranties, self-help, and weight-loss programs need to have no stocking level unless a limitation to the number of trainers available or class size exists. The biggest decision on these will be how you sell them. That will be discussed in the next chapter on promotion.

Who will show the customer how to use your product? Will you need to provide training so that the customer uses it effectively and safely while getting the most benefit from the product? If the user requires training, how will the training be delivered? You can use printed instructions or an online or compact disc video. They can be trained using in-person instruction either from one of your team members.

What additional upsale products can you sell that will enhance the user experience with your product? Having additional products and sales processes that encourage upsales assists your customers and increases your sales volume. You can use the upsales process like fast-food restaurants: sell a single item for $3.99 and then up-sell them to a meal instead with fries and a drink for $5.75. Or you can use the Amazon tactic: once the buyer has added an item to their cart, Amazon shows them 4 or 5 other items before checkout with the statement, *"Buyers of this product also purchased one of these items."* Either method of upsale is effective; however, neither will work if you do not incorporate an upsale process, train your team members, and ensure its use with every sale.

Will you offer a warranty, guarantee, or return policy? A 100% warranty including parts, labor, and shipping? A limited warranty on parts only? Will you offer a 30-, 60-, or 90-day money-back guarantee? For defects or product failure only? May the product be returned for any reason?

Now let's address pricing. With Internet searches and comparisons involved, in upward of 87% of all products purchased, similar products with wide variations in price and no discernable difference in quality will almost always have the customer default to the product with the lowest price. You can choose to offer your product for sale with the profit margin you decide, or you can offer it for a similar price as your competitor. If your product costs you $25 and you want to have a return of 300% then price it at $99.99. If your competitor sells a similar or the same product with no discernable difference in quality for $59.99, then that seller will sell 10 – 20 products for every one you sell. Here is the difference:

- Sell one with a $74.99 profit, or
- Sell ten with a $34.99 profit for a total of $349.90 or a 466% higher gross profit.
- Plus you get 10 customers available for upsales that you can also market to in the future via email.

Using the same example of a product that costs you $25 that you sell for $74.99, that the customer perceives is of better quality, that comes with a 30-day money-back guarantee and a $5 coupon that they can use toward a future purchase, you may sell 5 for every 10 they sell.

Here is the comparison:

- Sell 5 @ $74.99 with a $374.95 profit minus 1 return of $74.99 = $299,96; note the coupon will only impact the next sale, not this one, but it provides a greater incentive for the client to shop with you again. Or,
- Sell 10 @ $34.99 with a higher profit of $349.90 but no incentive for future sales.

Either sales program will work. Plus many other pricing variations exist as well. You must decide what you are the most comfortable with. Put that pricing in place and start selling!

SERVICES:

Like the list you made of your products, now list the services that you offer to your customers. Are these services associated with a product that you are selling? Services sold with your products are a great way to better serve your clients and increase your revenue. Are these services that you offer in conjunction with a product someone else is selling? Many companies sell products and software systems and then employ outside contractors to install their products and systems plus teach the clients how to use them. Are these services that you offer available online, at your facility, or at an off-site location such as the client's home or business? You may have the flexibility of more than one method to serve your client. For instance, if you offer training as a service:

- Price level 1: Training with a manual or other documents only.
- Price level 2: Online training via video with supporting documents.
- Price level 3: In-house training at your facility.
- Price level 4: On-site training at the client's location.

Next, let's identify your primary customers. Will they be Business to Business (B2B) clients? Or, will they be Business to Customer (B2C) or retail customers? Where are they located? Can they be identified or segmented by gender, age, education, geography, income, or previous ownership? Where will they be buying your services: at your facility, online, in person, or through a purchasing or human resources manager? Are you offering software as a service (SAAS)?

Narrowing down and identifying the best prospects for your services will impact staffing, online systems, and logistics. You need to decide what staffing levels are required to meet your servicing obligations. That will include both team members from your organization or from an outside vendor. The kinds of services you offer will also dictate what software you will need. Plus, you will need to decide in what geographical area you will offer your services.

How many sessions will be required for your services?

- One service session only, such as a delivery, setup, or installation.
- Sessions as requested by your clients, such as painters, plumbers, or carpet cleaners.
- Multiple recurring sessions daily, weekly, or monthly like facility cleaners, lawn or landscaping services, or pest control services.

How will you price your services? Similar to product pricing, a lot of service pricing information is online. You may use that information to price your services. However, unlike similar products which are similar commodities for price shoppers to compare, services are performed by people with varying degrees of skill. If your team members are all college or trade school educated but have little experience, you will not be able to price your services the same as services performed by technicians with an average of 20 years each serving customers, who continually upgrade their skill levels, and who represent a successful 40-year-old company.

Whether you are offering products, services, or both, how will you be paid? Numerous methods of payment are available. Your job is to complete the work and get paid on time. Payment options include cash or checks, credit or debit cards, cash apps like PayPal and Zelle, or bank transfers. Will you take trade-ins or bartered products or services for payment? If so, who will be accountable for valuing these trade-ins?

Next, let's consider the timing of your incoming payments. Will you collect upfront, like Amazon, before you deliver the product or service? Or will you be paid once the product is delivered or the service is performed such as occurs when buying new tires for your car? If you are offering payments monthly or in installments you have several options for collections:

- Submit bills monthly to be paid in full by the 10th of the next month.
- Installment payment plans with in-house financing with or without interest.
- Outside financing through a finance company, bank, or credit union. Be aware that if you use outside financing, you may have to discount the contract for the lender when they pay you. For instance, if the client purchases a $50,000 piece of machinery and puts $10,000 down, they will owe $40,000. If using an outside lender, they may charge you 1% – 1.5% to handle the contract. That would cost you between $400 – $600 for them to handle financing. Be sure to factor that in when dealing with an outside lender.

If you offer financing, be sure to assign responsibility to one person for the execution of the contract and the collection of funds either from the customer or an outside lender. Having a clear payment plan allows you to operate profitably while managing your cash flow and keeping both your clients and team members happy.

Once you have a firm grip on what you are selling, use the previous data from your operating statement to forecast how much you will sell, the revenue you expect, and the profit you project. Use the forecast guide in Chapter 6 for the process of forecasting.

If the items you are selling require storage of materials or finished products, you will need to develop a plan for distribution that involves stocking levels to control inventory levels. The best operations use computer models for "just-in-time" delivery of materials to you so you greatly reduce the amount of cash you have tied up in warehouses on or the shelves.

Let's pause for just a moment and get really deep in the weeds to analyze exactly what you are selling. Knowing this will help you identify your market and understand how to sell in your market.

As an e-commerce manager at a Savannah automobile dealership, we discovered that our primary vehicle buyer had the following characteristics:

- Average age: 20-45
- Average household income: $18K-$24K
- Average credit score: 530 in Equifax
- 50% had either no trade-in or a trade-in that was very un-

reliable or inoperable

- The vehicle they had or would be buying would be their only mode of getting to work, the doctor, to get groceries, etc. Without a vehicle, they were relying on friends, relatives, or public transportation—none of which was especially reliable.

Based on that information and a frank discussion that followed, we discovered that what we were selling was *"Freedom"*:

- Freedom to decide where you wanted to work and how much you could earn based on your mobility.
- Freedom to decide where you wanted to live by having reliable transportation.
- Freedom to take care of your family's needs by having reliable transportation.
- Freedom to build your credit by properly paying for a vehicle—a major piece of credit.
- Freedom of association based on having the ability to travel to a different church, organization, club, etc.

Once we understood how getting a better vehicle would improve the lives of our clients, we changed the in-house sales process to emphasize the *"Freedom"* that getting a new or newer vehicle from us would afford the client.

When you understand exactly what you are selling, you will sell more by taking better care of your clients with products and services that fit their needs.

CHAPTER 11: PROMOTION

Unfortunately, many organizations want to determine how and where to promote their products and services before determining either their go-to market strategy, who exactly they will market to, or what budget is available for promotion. We will discuss these in just a moment.

What is critically important is for the messaging to be exactly the <u>same for all media messaging platforms</u> so that there is <u>consistency</u> should your prospect view your message in more than one place, which is very likely.

For instance, if the item you are selling has a price of $119.95 on your website and the price in your facility is $149.95, it is easy to see how some dissatisfaction is created because of the price difference. It would be much better to show the original price of $149.95 in both places with a sale price of $119.95 now through Saturday. Moreover, this could also create some discriminatory liability should the item be online at $119.95 but you have it in a Spanish-speaking local newspaper for $149.95. Likewise, if you have a 15-day return policy online but do not honor this in your facility, you may create unnecessary ill will with your clients.

Always assume that your messages will reach your prospects on a minimum of 2 platforms.

Therefore, be consistent and straightforward with your messaging in order for your marketing to be effective.

Setting your marketing budget will require that you forecast how much you anticipate selling, the amount of gross profit to be created, and what percentage of gross profit you are comfortable investing to get those sales. You must determine what percentage of gross profit you will make available for the promotion.
For instance:

- 250 items projected to be sold at $500/each = <u>$125,000 in sales.</u>
- The cost of each sold item is $225; 250 x $225 = <u>$56,250 in cost.</u>
- Sales – cost = gross profit.

  o $125,000 - $56,250 = <u>$68,750 in gross profit.</u>

- If we use 12% of gross profit for promotion; $68,750 x 12% = an <u>$8250 promotional budget.</u>

Next, determine who are the best prospects for your products or services. Items to consider are age, gender, geographical location, household income, household size, education, prior purchases, etc. If your prospects are businesses, which types of businesses would get the most benefit from your product or service. Are you marketing only to subscription retailers like COSTCO or SAMS, or members of certain organizations such as labor unions, or certain types of businesses, or to the general public? Use the computation example shown above to determine your promotional budget. *(Bear in mind that the 12% of gross profit that was used above is an example and not a recommendation)*. Once you know who would need or want your product or service and you know your budget, you can now determine the most effective way to reach them.

- Online marketing allows you to target specific buyers/users. Email, Facebook, Twitter, Google, Pay-Per-Click (PPC), Amazon, your website, and affiliate marketing can get you in front of your prospects quickly and provide you with tools to measure your success over and beyond just knowing how much was sold.

- *VERY IMPORTANT...when designing your website or presenting your offer anywhere on the web be sure that you optimize for mobile devices. 7 out of 10 searches or website views are done on cell phones. Many times, web pages and offers published for a desktop do not convert well on the small screen if they are not optimized for mobile devices.*

- Newsletters, both in print and online, give you a great opportunity to market to existing clients and subscribers. These have a longer shelf life and get linked to, forwarded, and passed around because they provide other valuable or interesting information to the recipient in addition to your sales offer.

- Phone calls from a call center, either yours or one you contract with, can get you immediate and measurable results. However, you run the risk of being listed as spam, so your prospect may see a message from their caller ID such as *"Probable Spam"* before answering your call. Most prospects will not answer a call with this notification.

- Electronic marketing such as TV (both broadcast and cable) or radio (both station broadcasts and satellite) allows you to reach a much broader number of prospects but is harder to measure success.

- Print marketing such as newspapers, magazines, flyers, etc. have a longer shelf life and are most effective when mixed with other media.

- POP, point of purchase marketing, is used to sell and up-sell visitors to your facility or website.

You will have to decide the best avenues for presenting your products and services to the marketplace. Be sure to have your people, processes, products, or services in place before placing your marketing. You only have 1 chance to make a great 1st impression. That is why your first sale is the hardest for you. Once you deliver a great product or service, the door opens for you to continue building relationship with clients who are happy with their experience and your product or service.

Let's revisit the story from the last chapter about selling to sub-prime customers at a Savannah auto dealership. To successfully attack this market, we took advantage of several changes in our go-to market strategy. These changes facilitated success and increased sales. Hopefully, by knowing the steps we took, you can better identify your market and understand how to better present yourself to your customers.

Here is a quick review of the data that pushed us to revamp our go-to market strategy both in the showroom and in our marketing:

- Average age: 20 – 45

- Average household income: $18K – $28K

- Average credit score: 530 in Equifax

- 50% had either no trade-in or a trade-in that was very unreliable

- The vehicle they had or would be buying would be their only mode of getting to work, the doctor, to get groceries, etc. Without a vehicle, they were relying on friends, relatives, or public transportation

Based on that information and a frank discussion that followed, we discovered that what we were selling was *"Freedom"*:

- Freedom to decide where you wanted to work and how much you could earn based on your mobility.
- Freedom to decide where you wanted to live by having reliable transportation.
- Freedom to take care of your family's needs by having reliable transportation.
- Freedom to build your credit by properly paying for a vehicle—a major piece of credit.
- Freedom of association based on having the ability to travel to a different church, organization, club, etc.

Before making changes in our marketing, we shared this data with the entire sales team including sales managers, salespeople, and the call center (BDC) team. One key component of a successful campaign is to get all team members to understand the data. Then we used that as the basis for making the required sales process and marketing changes.

Step One was to redirect our sales presentation away from being primarily based on vehicle features, advantages, and benefits. Retraining all of our sales team members to sell the benefits of the *FREEDOMS* the buyer would gain by purchasing from us accomplished this.

Step Two was to create a short video that played on our website whenever the customer clicked on the "Bad Credit" tab in financing. The team members could also use this 15-second explanation video in the showroom or send the link to a prospective customer.

Step Three involved getting several more subprime lenders to arrange financing for these credit-challenged individuals.

Step Four was using a database program to understand which vehicles to sell based on the client's circumstances.

Step Five was a daily outreach to our Facebook followers who had responded to either today's ad or a Facebook ad from the last 30 days. Subprime customers require frequent contact, and Facebook is a great place for daily contact.

Step Six was placing our subprime ads for radio and TV on stations and times when these prospective customers would be listening or viewing.

Note that the internal changes happened first, and the changes in marketing followed. Process changes <u>always</u> come before marketing changes. Now, let's do an exercise.

1. Identify and write down a client group that you have not effectively been able to assist in taking advantage of one or more of your products or services? Be specific.
2. Are your people trained to effectively sell or service that group of people? If not, what training is required to get them ready to assist these clients?

3. How can you use your website and Facebook pages to reach these prospects?

4. How much additional revenue may be generated by these changes? Use your forecast to guide you.

5. From where can you redirect funds, or are there additional funds available, to market to this group? How much can you allocate?

6. After your internal changes have been made and your marketing adjusted or augmented, be sure to track your performance.

Here are a couple of test questions you should ask yourself before utilizing any method of advertising:

- If using video or audio to promote your business, close your eyes and listen to the words of the presentation. Will that electronic message create a mental picture for your target audience? Does the video presentation assist in creating that mental picture for your prospect?

- What benefits of using your product or service will the client visualize from your ad?

- Do your video or audio messages promote those benefits?

- Does your messaging mirror what your client will find online?

- Does your messaging mirror what your client will encounter when they visit your location?

If using billboard advertising:

- Can your message be read and understood in 7 seconds? Read time must be 7 seconds maximum.

- Does your message contain more than 7 words? A message should be 7 words maximum.

- If using an image or picture, are you using more than one? Do not use more than one image or picture.

- Can the image be understood in 7 seconds? Should be 7 seconds mamimum.

- Since most billboards are best utilized for directional information, do not use more than 7 words.

For Point-of-Purchasing (POP) advertising:

- Is this for the products or services you are selling on other media?

  o i.e., a special promotion so the client will know immediately that they came to the correct location. This is a comforting non-verbal statement that what they heard is both correct and available.

- Is this for an upsale or add-on product or service?

  o i.e., a big sandwich with fries and a drink for a higher price?
  o i.e., a maintenance or extended warranty with an auto purchase?

- Is this to plant a seed with your client who came in for one thing to consider a separate product or service?

  - Client has their car in for service and sees a sign stating: *"We want to buy your car! See Nicole for information."*
  - Client is in your clothing or book store and sees a sign stating: *"Join us next door for a half-priced latte or espresso with your purchase here today of $25 or more!"*

One last question before we leave promotion and marketing:

"What is your positioning or branding statement in 20 words or less?"

____

____

Here are some examples:

- A positioning statement favorably places you as a better alternative versus others with whom you compete.

  - Wheaties: *"The Breakfast of Champions!"*

- A branding statement will automatically bring your organization to your prospect's mind.

- o **Nike:** *"Just do it!"*

- Some statements are great in that they do both.

- o **M&M's:** *"Melts in your mouth, not in your hand!"*

If you can compress your organization's brand into 15 words or less, you will be miles ahead of your competition.

- ____
- ____

The next section will provide you with a step-by-step process for forecasting and action plans to build a consistently high-performing team.

SECTION FOUR:
STEPS FOR YOUR ACTION
PLAN

CHAPTER 12: ACTION PLAN STEP ONE—FORECASTING

Your organizational action plan will begin with your forecast for an average month and for the next year. Each department needs to develop its forecast. To do that, leaders need data—lots of data. Let's examine how this can be done by using some examples from an automobile dealership. We will use data from the October operation statement. For your business, you can break down the information by department, sales category, location, etc. Just be sure that you can forecast that group using the data that you have available.

For a new vehicle sales department with 4 models, get the data for each model. For this example, we will use YTD information for the previous 10 months.

New vehicle department: Gross profit calculations from the October operating statement:

- Model Alpha

  - Current year through 10 months:

    - 200 Units / 10 months = 20 sales per month
    - $4,800,000 sales / 10 months = $480,000 sales per month
    - $4,500,000 cost / 10 months = $450,000 cost per month
    - <u>(Sales – Cost = Sales Gross Profit) = $30,000 per month</u>
    - $320,000 finance gross profit / 10 months = $32,000 per month
    - <u>SALES GROSS + FINANCE GROSS = $62,000 per month</u>

- Model Beta:

  - Current year through 10 months:

    - 240 Units / 10 months = 24 sales per month
    - $8,400,000 sales / 10 months = $840,000 sales per month
    - $7,560,000 cost / 10 months = $756,000 cost per month
    - <u>(Sales – Cost = Sales Gross Profit) = $84,000 per month</u>

- - $384,000 finance gross profit / 10 months = $38,400 per month
  - <u>SALES GROSS + FINANCE GROSS = $122,400 per month</u>

- Model Charlie:

  - Current year through 10 months:

    - 80 Units / 10 months = 8 sales per month
    - $3,600,000 sales / 10 months = $360,000 sales per month
    - $3,280,000 cost / 10 months = $328,000 cost per month
    - <u>(Sales – Cost = Sales Gross Profit) = $32,000 per month</u>
    - $128,000 finance gross profit / 10 months = $12,800 per month
    - <u>SALES GROSS + FINANCE GROSS = $44,800 per month</u>

- Model Delta:

  - Current year through 10 months:

    - 180 Units / 10 months = 18 sales per month
    - $3,510,000 sales / 10 months = $351,000 sales per month

- $3,366,000 cost / 10 months = $336,600 cost per month
- <u>(Sales – Cost = Sales Gross Profit) = $15,000 per month</u>
- $324,000 finance gross profit / 10 months = $32,400 per month
- <u>SALES GROSS + FINANCE GROSS = $47,400 per month</u>

- Total Gross Profit for New Vehicle Department Calculation

    o $62,000 Alpha
    o $122,400 Beta
    o $44,800 Charlie
    o <u>$47,400 Delta</u>
    o $276,600 GROSS PROFIT FOR NEW VEHICLE DEPARTMENT PER MONTH

New vehicle department expense calculation from October operating statement:

- Payroll Expense

    o $497,888 payroll expense / 10 months = $49,788 per month

- Semi-Fixed Expense

- $744,800 semi-fixed expense / 10 months = $74,480 per month

- Fixed Expense

  - $608,520 fixed expense /10 months = $60,852 per month
  - $1,851,200 TOTAL EXPENSE PER MONTH / 10 MONTHS = $185,120 PER MONTH

New vehicle department current year average month net profit:

- $276,600 gross profit
- <u>-$185,120 expenses</u>
- $91,480 NET PROFIT FORECAST PER MONTH

The above calculation is designed to show you and your managers how to calculate an <u>average month</u> for the <u>current year.</u> This is made easy when using the October operating statement by dividing every YTD entry on the statement by 10 to get an average month. Do this for every line item for every department in your organization until you have what an average month shows for this year. In the retail auto dealership business, November is usually a little less than the average and December is a little more than average, thus using the October statement to calculate an average month is usually accurate.

The reason for getting the data reduced to an average month is so we can project future sales and expenses in an average month for next year. We will use that average month for this year to forecast changes to each entry for the coming year.

Here is an example once again using the average month for this year factoring in some projections for next year:

- Model Alpha selling 23 units per month with the same average gross profit:

    - $62,000 gross profit / 20 units = $3,100/unit last year
    - 23 units times $3,100 avg gross profit = $71,300 Alpha gross forecast

- Model Beta selling 25 units per month with the same average gross profit:

    - $122,400 gross profit / 24 sales = $5,100/unit last year
    - 25 units times $5,100 avg gross profit = $127,500 Beta gross forecast

- Model Charlie selling 25 units per month with the same average gross profit:

    - $44,800 gross profit / 8 units = $5,600/unit last year
    - 25 units times $5,600 avg gross profit = $140,000 Charlie gross profit

- Model Delta selling 21 units per month with the same average gross profit

- o $47,400 gross profit / 18 units = $2,633/unit last year
  - o 21 units times $2,633 avg gross profit = $55,293 Delta gross profit

- Total new vehicle department Gross Profit Forecast:

  - o $71,300 Alpha gross profit forecast
  - o $127,500 Beta gross profit forecast
  - o $140,000 Charlie gross profit forecast
  - o $55,293 Delta gross profit forecast
  - o $394,033 TOTAL AVERAGE MONTHLY GROSS PROFIT FORECAST

- Payroll Expense increases to 19% of gross profit

  - o $49,788 expense / $276,600 gross profit = 18% payroll this year
  - o $394,033 gross forecast times 19% = $74,866 payroll expense forecast

- Semi-fixed Expense increases to 27.5% of gross profit

  - o $74,480 expense / $276,600 gross profit = 26.9% semi-fixed this year
  - o $394,033 gross forecast times 27.5% = $108,359 semi-fixed expense forecast

- Fixed Expense to remain at current percentage of gross profit

- o $60,852 expense / $276,600 = 22% fixed expense this year
- o $394,033 gross forecast times 22% = <u>$86,687 fixed expense forecast</u>

- Total new vehicle department Expense Forecast:

  - o $74,866 payroll expense forecast
  - o $108,359 semi-fixed expense forecast
  - o <u>$86,687 fixed expense forecast</u>
  - o $269,912 TOTAL AVERAGE MONTHLY EXPENSE FORECAST

- Average new vehicle department Profit Forecast:

  - o Gross profit forecast minus expense forecast = net profit average month
  - o <u>$394,033 GROSS PROFIT - $269,912 EXPENSE = $124,121 NET PROFIT FORECAST FOR AN AVERAGE MONTH</u>

Your forecast for each department will be configured the same way. Using your October operating statement:

- Compute the average monthly gross profit for each department

  - o Use the expected changes to forecast the average monthly gross profit for next year

- Compute the average monthly expenses for each department

    o   Use the expected changes to forecast the average monthly expense for next year

- Compute the average monthly net profit for each department

    o   Use the expected changes to forecast the average monthly net profit for next year

- Add all the department numbers together for your total average monthly forecast

Let's summarize this by having you do an exercise. Pick out a department or a team and fill in these boxes:

- $\$$___________ Current Average Monthly Sales
- $\$$___________ Current Average Monthly Expenses
- $\$$___________ Current Average Profit or Loss

What can you do in the short term to improve these numbers a

- Sales:

    - ____
    - ____
    - ____

- Expenses:

    - ____
    - ____
    - ____

- With these changes, you will forecast new numbers:

    - $\$$___________ Forecast Average Monthly Sales
    - $\$$___________ Forecast Average Monthly Expenses
    - $\$$___________ Forecast Average Monthly Profit or Loss

In Chapter 13, we will examine the PEOPLE section of your action plan.

CHAPTER 13: ACTION PLAN STEP TWO—PEOPLE

The second step in putting together your action plan to achieve your forecast may give you some heartburn. If you are the kind of leader who does all the planning for your team alone and then expects the team to execute your plan, this section may make you uneasy.

I understand! I get it!

There was a time when I expected that I would do all the planning because I was the one who had to answer for the success or failure of the endeavor. I wanted total control of the process. What I did not understand was that the process was controlling me. Once I realized that it was possible to actually get help, the concrete blocks fell off my shoulders because the team wanted to win as much as I did.

Getting your team involved provides some very positive outcomes.

- By sharing the forecast, each team member knows where the goalpost is. They know that they share individually and collectively in the success or failure in meeting the forecast.

- Getting the team involved early creates "buy-in" for the processes that the team decides on. Because they have bought into an action plan that they helped to create, they will push hard to achieve the forecast. When team members participate in the action plan they feel valued for their ideas as well as their work efforts.

- By participating in the formation of the action plan, team members understand who will be held responsible for the team's success and how they share in that accountability. This creates a strong incentive for each member to ensure that the action plan is properly designed, communicated, and executed.

- If you intend to grow your business, then you will need team members to step up and accept more responsibility. Those who do will advance and help your organization succeed and grow.

Organize a team meeting with your people to share the details of the forecast and explain the shared responsibility that all members have to meet or exceed their numbers. If you have a very large team, then get the team leaders together to help you with the details of how to achieve your forecast.

With your team, you need to answer the question of how many team members it will take to meet your financial objectives. You will have some who want the extra help because they feel they cannot do any more. And, you will have some salespeople who believe that by adding extra salespeople they will sell less and make less money.

Here is an example: assume a retail automobile sales department with 8 salespersons averaging 82 sales per month this year. Next year your forecast is to sell 100 vehicles per month. Some of your current salespeople may object to the addition of 2 extra salespeople. This is because they assume that there exists only enough traffic to sell 80 – 82 units per month. This allows you to share the following:

- For 10 months we have had 8 salespeople and they averaged 82 sales per month.
- Your marketing budget is being increased by 10% per month so you will have additional funds to attract new business.
- Your inventory level will increase by 20% to enable the extra 18 – 20 vehicle sales per month.
- You have engaged a social media trainer to teach them how they can boost their sales volume with effective individual efforts online with Facebook, Instagram, and YouTube.
- The industry average for auto salespeople is 10 per month. To get the extra 18 – 20 sales per month, you will need to add 2 salespeople.

Even if they do not initially agree with adding more salespeople, they will appreciate your listening to their issues and explaining the rationale behind expanding the team.

Just for fun, let's assume that your team of 8 salespersons is only selling 68 vehicles per month. You tell them that you will be adding 3 new salespeople to achieve the 100 units per month in your forecast. You use the same bullet points to explain what you are doing with inventory and marketing. Then you let them know that you will help them with the additional training to help them reach their 10-unit quota. Now the pressure is on them to improve. This is quite different from simply stating you would hire 3 new salespeople to meet the 100 unit per month quota for the team giving no explanations.

This applies not just to salespeople. It applies to all teams. How many team members are needed to meet your objective? Are their people available to promote or transfer from within other teams in the organization? How many do you need to hire? What skills are necessary to achieve success in meeting the forecast? Who will be responsible for recruiting these people? What training is required to get the new hires up to speed as quickly as possible? Who will train them? To have a real goal, the people part of your action plan should look like this:

- Hire 1 new lube tech by February 1, 2022. They should have basic tech school training before starting and the ability to begin training in brakes, tires, and tune-ups under the direction of Derrick, our master technician. Bob, the shop foreman is responsible for filling this position.
- Hire 1 new service adviser by March 1, 2022. This person will spend the 1st week training with our service drive foreman, George, who will be responsible for filling this position.

Be sure to use the SMART requirements for your people goals:

- Specific
- Measurable
- Accountable
- Realistic
- Timely

Next, review your staff scheduling to ensure that you have the best possible staffing to achieve your forecast. Coordinate scheduling with other departments or teams, so that by coordinating activities, all team members become more productive. Measure productivity so that all team members will see what the others produce. For instance: If the Alpha Service Team with one adviser and three technicians has a daily productivity goal of 40 hours completed and billed, post the following message in your internal messaging and on the wall showing:

- Nancy, service adviser, sold 52 hours; 12 are awaiting parts
- Luke, service tech, completed 15 hours and has 9 hours awaiting parts
- Amos, lube tech, competed 7 hours and has 0 hours awaiting parts
- Sam, service tech, completed 14 hours and has 6 hours awaiting parts

Using this example:

- Nancy will be all over the parts manager to get the needed parts
- Luke will be on Amos to do his share to meet the team's daily quota
- Amos knows he needs to get it together to produce his 10 hours per day
- Sam offers to help Amos so he can get his productivity up

Posting this information for all to see is how you get buy-in from team members. Plus, they make each other more accountable to meet the team objective. This synergy is much more productive than simply telling the team what the plan is while they had no input in creating the plan.

As you involve your team members in producing the action plans to meet your forecast, be sure to ask for their input and suggestions on how to make the team more productive and serve their customers better. When getting their input, require that they use Dale Carnegie's 4 rules for discussing topics during these sessions:

1. Clearly describe the problem in your own words.
2. Clearly describe what you think caused the problem.
3. Describe the options available to correct the issue.
4. Which option do you recommend and why?

With team members understanding that this process in compulsory, you will avoid team meetings becoming complaint sessions. This is because the individuals bring forward every suggestionor issue to be discussed using this 4-rule format.

If you have not already done so, review the personality profiles of the individuals who will be participating in these sessions. Knowing how the participants communicate and process information will help you, as the leader, to keep the discussion moving forward and promote actionable decisions. Keep in mind that disagreement is good and forces your team members to understand that there may be more, different, and possibly better ways to approach and solve problems. Productive meetings will help participants grow in knowledge. Plus, their leadership skills will increase as you grow your bench, allowing your organization to improve and expand.

This is a great time to review all team members' job descriptions and update those that need improvement. Print these descriptions and have all team members review and sign them. These actions will remind team members of what is currently expected of them or change their responsibilities to either add to or update what their positions now require. The leader's responsibility is to keep team members focused on the tasks and objectives at hand. Use these job descriptions to maintain focus on why and how important their successful and timely completion of tasks will bring about the achievement of the team's overall objectives.

Last, but most importantly, examine the compensation programs that you have for your team members and leaders.

- Do they reward exceptional accomplishments?
- Do they encourage achievement of the forecast?
- Do they overpay for average performance?
- Do your team members truly understand how they are paid?
- What effect will changing compensation plans have on your team effort?

All-in-all, always start your action plans with your people. They are your most valuable asset!

In the next chapter, we will discuss how systems and processes will either help or hinder the team effort to achieve the team forecast.

CHAPTER 14: ACTION PLAN STEP THREE—PROCESSES AND SYSTEMS

For effective action plans, we need to examine your team's successful processes and systems, take advantage of the opportunities to improve those that must be improved, and look for new processes that are required to meet changing opportunities or solve problems.

Sports teams use game and practice films to examine their team's processes. They also use films of their opponents to decide how to adjust their actions to either improve what they are doing or develop new processes needed to meet upcoming challenges.

- How has the RPO, run-pass-option, changed the way football teams use their offenses and how the defenses deploy to thwart them?

- How have basketball offenses and defenses changed with the 3-point line added to encourage long-range shots?
- How has the "transfer portal" changed the way college football recruiters work as they seek to improve the talent levels at all positions.

The military uses After Action Reports and analysis to confirm the effectiveness of their plans, tactics, and overall strategy. They make changes and order retraining to protect against repeating past mistakes and to take advantage of changing strategic issues and battlefield tactics of their opponents. Both our military and those of our adversaries also require changes in answer to updated technology and weapon systems.

- **How did the military change tactics when chemical weapons were first deployed in World War I in Europe?**
- **How did the use of railroads for troop movement and deployment change the way that armies approached or fled the battlefield in the American Civil War?**
- **Why does the military employ tactics to *"adapt and overcome"* to win battles?**

If sports teams and the military accept that change is inevitable, requiring them to commit to continuous improvement, does it not make sense that the same attitude is required in business, academics, service organizations, and government? Is not change and improvement required to utilize updated technology, new products and services, and changes in the skill levels of team members?

I submit to you that continuous improvement and the attitude to *"adapt and overcome"* must infuse every organization.

Here is an effective exercise to use as your teams endeavor to include process changes in their action plans. During your team session, have the attendees list some processes that either need improving or changing completely.

1. _______________________________________
2. _______________________________________
3. _______________________________________

With your list completed, have a frank discussion about how to update or change those processes to meet current conditions. Then put those changes into your action plan.

Next, list the processes that are currently very effective in achieving your team goals.

1. _______________________________________
2. _______________________________________
3. _______________________________________

Are all your team members trained in these processes? If not, why not? Include process training in your action plan.

This next step will involve either internal or external organizations or committees committed to continuous improvement. These groups find and publish lists of *best practices* for your organization and organizations like yours. You can discover these *best practices* in trade publications, meeting notes, newsletters, after-campaign reports, and websites. Review these *best practices* with your team to decide whether one or more of them may help your team meet or exceed their goals. Some of these can make your efforts more effective. Some of them guide you to take advantage of new opportunities. Either way, these *best practices* can provide you with a world of opportunities for improvement.

As you examine your systems and processes, be sure to complete these action items.

- List the *"core processes"* without which you cannot function nor succeed in your objectives.
- List the *best practices* to use for your organization.
- As you execute changes or add new processes, be sure to publish both timelines for their implementation and who will be accountable for meeting those objectives.
- There must be a system in place to regularly review both systems and processes to ensure that what your team is using is effective to meet your team goals and is the best process or system for the budget you have available

CHAPTER 15: ACTION PLAN STEP FOUR—PRODUCTS AND SERVICES

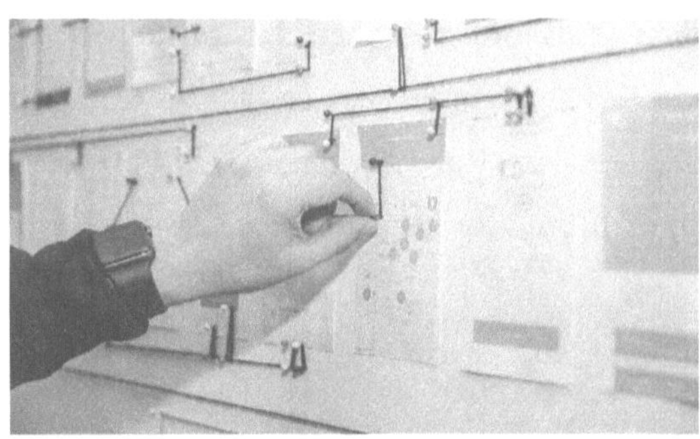

To keep your team focused on successfully meeting or exceeding your forecast goals, it is imperative to clearly define what products and/or services you are providing for your clients.

Here is how this would look for a new vehicle dealership:

- New Vehicle Department:

    o Sell models Alpha, Beta, Charlie, and Delta to assist clients in meeting their objective of getting a new vehicle.
    o Assist with their trade-in.
    o Assist in providing financing.
    o Sell accessories to help the client better enjoy or make more useful the vehicle that they are buying.
    o Complete the setup of all the systems in the vehicle for use by the clients.

o   Ensure that clients know how to use all the systems in their new vehicle.

- Used Vehicle Department:

  o   Sell pre-owned cars, trucks, vans, or SUVs to assist clients in meeting their objective of getting a used vehicle.
  o   Assist with their trade-in.
  o   Assist in providing financing.
  o   Sell accessories to help the client better enjoy or make more useful the vehicle that they are buying.
  o   Complete the setup of all the systems in the vehicle for use by the clients.
  o   Ensure that their clients know how to use all the systems in their new vehicle.

- Finance Department:

  o   Arrange acceptable financing for clients buying vehicles to include negotiating with lenders for the best terms available.
  o   Process the required paperwork for the transaction:

    - Titling the purchased vehicle.
    - Getting the trade-in out of the client's name.
    - Paying off the trade-in and getting the title.
    - Issuing a temporary license plate for the purchased vehicle.

- o Provide product options for protection for the client and enhanced use of the vehicle.
- o Provide maintenance options for the client, making interaction with the service and parts teams easier and less expensive.
- o Apply for refunds of financial products sold by the dealership.

- Service Department:

  - o Understand the needs of clients and their vehicles.
  - o Provide necessary warranty repairs for vehicles as prescribed by the manufacturer and warranty company.
  - o Interface with manufacturers and warranty companies to get all the benefits they provide.
  - o Coordinate with the parts department to obtain the correct parts for the client's vehicle.
  - o Recommend maintenance for the client's vehicle to ensure safe operation, optimal fuel economy, and longevity of service.
  - o Refer clients to the finance department for protection products to enhance ownership of the vtall accessories on the client's vehicle.
  - o Provide new vehicle inspection and processing for the new vehicle department.
  - o Provide used vehicle processing and reconditioning for used vehicles.

- Parts Department:

    o Establish and utilize an effective stock level of parts and accessories for customers and new and used vehicle department clients.
    o Sell accessories and replacement parts to clients, the service department, and the vehicle sales departments.
    o Ensure that parts sold qualify for warranty payments from the manufacturer and warranty companies.

This example of an automobile dealership allows all team members and clients to understand what they sell, provide, or service.

Let's look at your organization:

- What products are you selling?

    o Are there some that need to be phased out?
    o What products will you add to better serve your clients?

- What services is your organization providing?

    o Are there some services that need to be eliminated?
    o What services can you offer to better serve your clients?

Ensure that your facilities are set up to effectively display your products and services. Use your team meetings to identify opportunities for changes in your displays and the products or services you offer. Sometimes small changes can create massive new opportunities. Here are some examples:

- The 3M company had team members in Minnesota putting glue on small scraps of paper to be used in their workstations. The Post-It Note was launched and created a new set of products that they could offer customers.

- Auto loan terms grew from an average of 24 months to 72 months because buyers needed the longer terms to keep payments in line with their budgets. This meant that a large number of buyers owned cars where their loan payoffs were greater than the value of their vehicles. Clients experiencing total losses due to wrecks or theft who owed more on their loan than the value of their vehicles were experiencing insurance settlements that did not pay off the entire loans. They could not get a new auto loan until the old loan was paid off, putting these clients at a great disadvantage when trying to replace their wrecked vehicle. Insurance companies and auto dealers began offering GAP policies on vehicle loans to ensure their loans would be paid off if a client experienced a total loss and their insurance company did not pay off their loan.

These are just 2 examples of expanding customer offerings to meet customer needs. What products or services can you make available to your clients to create added value or help solve a problem?

Last, ensure that every team member knows what part they play in delivering superior service and a fantastic product to your clients.

One very effective way to accomplish this communication both to and from your team members is to establish a team member-only *"Continuous Improvement Team"* or committee. (When Saturn Corporation was still part of General Motors, each Saturn dealership had an *"Achieving Customer Enthusiasm" (ACE) team.)* Your team should be made up of team members chosen by their peers who meet regularly, monthly, or bimonthly to discuss problems needing correction and opportunities to take advantage of.

Every department should be represented. I recommend that each team member on the committee serve for 6 months with half coming off every 3 months. A member of management should attend not to lead the meeting but to answer questions and keep the discussion productive. This team of elected representative members should be charged with making recommendations to management for improvements and requesting clarification of any issues. Issues to be discussed must follow the Dale Carnegie rules for making recommendations or discussing issues. These 4 steps must be followed:

1. Describe the problem or opportunity completely.
2. List the issues that caused the problem or opportunity.
3. List all the options that may correct the problem or allow the team to take advantage of the opportunity.
4. State which option you support and why.

Using this process keeps the discussion productive and leads to recommendations not just discussions.

The manager who attends may answer questions or commit to getting answers for the team. That person does not run the meeting. This representative team will choose its own leader to facilitate the meetings.

List all the changes the team will make in your action plans. Be sure to include timelines for completion and who is responsible for ensuring these products or services are added or deleted.

In Chapter 16 we will discuss the action plans for promotion.

CHAPTER 16: ACTION PLAN STEP FIVE—PROMOTION

In discussing how to successfully promote your organization, use your action plan as a guide to getting the most exposure while staying within your budget. Let's start with your forecast. There are many different ways to budget for marketing and more ways to advertise than you can ever use. In the real world, you have to decide which budgeting method is best for you.

In a business with high-priced items, you may use a dollar amount per unit sold. For instance, if you are selling vehicles, you may assign a dollar amount per the number of units you have forecasted to sell. If your average monthly forecast is to sell 150 vehicles and your expected investment is $400 per vehicle, your budget for your average month would be $60,000.

If you prefer to use a percentage of gross profit and you forecast a gross profit of $1800 per unit, your gross profit would be $270,000. If you have budgeted 20% of gross profit, then $270,000 times 20% is $54,000. Either method will work. The key to effective budgeting is to be consistent.

If you anticipate lower than average sales due to a shorter month and expected bad weather, then you will want to reduce your unit sales forecast and gross profit for that month. That action will also reduce your marketing forecast using either formula.

If you are selling thousands of lower-priced items under $100, it may be best to use a percentage of expected gross profit as your guide for budgeting. If you expect to sell 100,000 items with an average price of $25, your sales would be $2,500,000. At a forecasted gross profit of 50% of sales, you would gain $1,250,000 in gross profit. With an ad budget of 2% of gross profit, your budget would be $25,000. Once again, the key is to be consistent in how you budget for marketing.

Let's pause for just a moment. I am not advocating for $400 per unit sold, 20% of gross profit, or 2% of gross profit. These were mere examples for illustrative purposes only. What I am sharing is that you must have a method for forecasting how much you will spend on promotion. Plus, you need to be consistent in your planning.

Trade organizations are very good at sharing best practices to help you plan your budget for promotion. Grocers, big-box retailers, online marketers, auto repair shops, jewelry stores, restaurants, etc. all have active trade associations or industry groups that can guide you in how to budget and how much to budget. Use their *best practices* to budget for marketing in your forecast.

Next, let's address co-op funds available from manufacturers. These create a pool of money based on either how much you buy from them or how much you sell of their product. Co-op funds may be used to augment or reduce your promotional budget. However, there are usually strict rules on how and where you can use these funds. Plus, the manufacturer will have a strict program for reimbursement.
For example:

- The manufacturer says you can get $.10 per unit if you buy 25,000 units or $2500.
- They further stipulate that you must spend at least $10,000 to qualify for the $2500 reimbursement.
- They further require that the ads meet their marketing standards and that this applies to newspaper ads only.
- Finally, you must submit actual ads showing the dates that the ad ran and a notarized affidavit from the newspaper stating that the ad ran on those dates. Plus, you must apply within 45 days of when the ads ran to qualify.

If you do not follow their exact rules, then you will not receive your $2500. However, if you are okay with the rules, and your ads are effective, it is great to receive a $2500 refund on your $10,000 investment. Smart operators use these funds to augment their ad budgets or reduce their expenses. To ensure compliance, follow these necessary practices:

- Make sure that one trusted person in your organization will be the champion for your co-op campaigns and for co-op funds collection.

- I would not use your ad agency because in the event you change agencies, your co-op funds could be lost due to non-compliance.
- Budget for these funds monthly so accounting will be flagged if they have been applied for but have not been received promptly.

Please allow me to mention one very important step before we proceed on how to use your forecasted promotional funds. If your organization produces a monthly operating statement (recommended), you need to know that most bills for marketing do not arrive before the middle of the next month after the scheduled run. Assuming that your accounting manager is tasked with producing the monthly statement by the 5th business day of the next month, these bills will not arrive until after the statement has been produced. This means you have a choice:

- Expense the marketing bills in the month they are received—next month. This means that your operating statement will show the expense that you budgeted for this month on next month's statement.
- Or, produce your ad budget for this month and have your accounting manager set up this month's anticipated expenses as prepaid debits. When the bills come in next month that manager will clean up the prepaid marketing expense schedule, making adjustments if necessary. This process means that what you forecast to spend this month will be expensed in the correct month.

Now, with your monthly promotional forecast in hand, you need to decide where best to invest your funds. In Chapter 11 we discussed the benefits and drawbacks of different forms of marketing. You must decide the best avenues for promoting your organization. Use historical data from your past campaigns, best practices, industry information, plus the availability of co-op funds to promote your event or business. Here are a couple of tips to stretch your funds and get the best value:

1. On your promotional calendar, set up the dates for your biggest events. Here are some suggestions:
    a. January: Winter white sale in the last half of the month.
    b. February: Capture the tax refund buyers at mid-month.
    c. March: St. Patrick's Day with a green theme (green money savings).
    d. April: Easter or spring sale or baseball opening event.
    e. May: Memorial Day pre-vacation event (2nd best sale of the year).
    f. June: Beginning of summer vacation specials.
    g. July: Back to school sales.
    h. August: End of summer sale.
    i. September: Labor Day sale.
    j. October: Octoberfest sale.
    k. November: Spooky or Halloween sale.
    l. December: End of the year sale.

2. For electronic media, plus having your yearly major campaigns set up, use your annual promotional budget to determine an average month for the entire year. Decide how much of that will be spent on TV and radio. Then negotiate with these media, letting them know that you will place your order for the entire year so you want the best rates based on the fact that they are selling an entire year's schedule. Believe me, they will drop their rates drastically knowing that they just sold an entire year of advertising.

3. If the year is an election year, be sure to insist that they charge you the same as the political ad rate. Politicians have set up laws to dictate that they pay the absolute lowest rates. Insist that you get that rate. If they will not comply, cancel your scheduled advertising spots and choose another media source.

4. Use your Facebook page:

   a. Encourage visitors to your FB page to follow you on Facebook. Have a monthly drawing of all followers for a $100 coupon that can be used to buy your products or services.

   b. Post new ads 4 – 5 days per week. Boost the ads with $10 – $20. You will be amazed at how much you can get with this small expenditure.

   c. If you have salespeople, have them send congratulations for purchases from their Facebook pages and tag your site. They can also broadcast special events and sales through their pages. This is very effective and costs you nothing.

5. Use an email company or your CRM software vendor to send out twice-monthly newsletters. Be sure that the majority of the newsletter is reserved for interesting and helpful information, so it does not appear to be just another sales letter and gets reported as spam. Readers will appreciate information that is relevant to them personally. But they will block you if all they ever see are sales ads.

6. On your website. You already paid for this, so make it more effective:

    a. Run contests to create interest and excitement.

    b. Use the FAQ section to provide helpful information.

    c. Encourage readers to ask questions—then answer them. If you get a lot of readers asking the same question, then use the answer as a special article in your newsletter.

    d. Have links for special savings leading to a "squeeze" page that creates a lead for your staff to follow up. The "squeeze" page collects their name and contact information for your staff to follow up on.

    e. Share information about your products and services so visitors can make informed decisions regarding what they will purchase or lease.

7. Be sure to use your *"Google My Business"* (GMB) page effectively:

    a. Be sure all the information is accurate.

    b. Be sure to claim the name and location of each

business that you operate at that location. For instance, if you have *Bob's Dry Cleaning* and **also** *Mary's Alterations* at the same address, be sure that you claim both.

c. Answer all reviews within 24 hours.

    i. Thanking people for their 4- and 5-star reviews.

    ii. Share that a manager will contact those who have posted less than positive reviews and ensure that a manager follows up. Then post the results back on Google.

Track the effectiveness of your marketing for every promotion. Use the data to make decisions on future marketing. The best measure of the effectiveness of a promotion is based on the number of units sold and expressed per sale. For instance, if you sold 800 units with a $10,000 budget your cost per sale (CPS) is $12.50. Many online media companies insist on using a cost-per-click to measure the effectiveness of a promotion. Using the same budget of $10,000 that generates 4000 click-throughs, they would report a cost per click (CPC) of only $2.50. That is helpful for the ad company but does not realistically show how you benefited from your ad investment. I recommend that you use the CPS to measure the effectiveness of your campaigns because that computation more accurately reflects the benefits you received from your marketing investment.

Last, in the formulation of your promotional action plans, ensure that the messages your prospective customers see are exactly the same. Clearly stated, this means that the message you are promoting at any given time is the same across ALL media. Mixed messages are not only confusing for your prospective customers, they reduce the number of times that these prospects hear or see the same message. To achieve maximum effectiveness, the prospect should be exposed to the exact same message a minimum of 3 times. For example, the prospect hears a radio ad for a widget at $9.99. They search your website and get the same message. Then they go to Amazon and see the same message. This not only makes your message effective, but it also allows a trust to be established between you and your prospect. Imagine after all that same messaging, this same prospect comes to your location and finds the widget priced at $12.99. Would that prospect be pleased? Surprised? Disappointed? Feel betrayed? What sort of review will that prospect leave on Google, Yelp, Amazon, or on your website? Keep your messaging the same on ALL platforms.

In Chapter 17, we will discuss how to use reviews of your action plans and forecasts and how to make the required adjustments.

CHAPTER 17: ACTION PLAN STEP SIX—REVIEW AND ADJUST

Every team, organization, or business has the basic and necessary requirement of assessing where they performed relative to their forecast. Regularly review your team's performance—preferably weekly or monthly and at least every quarter. If you are using the average monthly forecast as the basis for comparison, compare your actual results versus the forecasted numbers. If you are using *best practice* numbers from your trade group, how did your performance compare with those who are at the top of their game? If you are comparing your numbers to the group's average performance benchmarks, how do you measure up? If you come up short, do not panic. Take a sober, realistic look and start looking for areas of opportunity.

If your review shows that you are on track, then celebrate because all wins deserve to be recognized and applauded. Do not underestimate the value of celebration. To say, *"We hit the forecast. That's what we were expected to do. Why celebrate just doing our jobs?"*

is easy. Using that observation with that attitude nullifies all the work that went into the team's achievements. It is better to say, *"Fantastic! We hit our goals this month! Congratulations to all! Thank you for a great job!"* Remember, your team takes its cues from you. When you acknowledge and celebrate winning, you will get more winning to celebrate!

After hitting your numbers and celebrating, then observe those areas in which you can improve. Share improvement strategies with individual team members. Ask them how they think <u>we</u> can do better. Ask them what <u>they</u> can do better. Let them know that you are committed to *continuous improvement* for yourself and for them as well.

Let me pause for a moment to mention CBE from Pat Riley's book, *The Winner Within.* Coach Riley describes a program that utilized *"Career Best Effort"* or CBE. This strategy asks each player to increase their performance by just 1% over their previous monthly effort. Tracking performance and having that commitment, with Pat Riley as their head coach, they won 5 NBA championships. The key was tracking each player with 5 basic measures of performance from month to month. Instead of comparing the player against other players, they were compared against their own performance from the previous month. When someone is compared against himself, coupled with the commitment to achieve a 1% improvement in their month-to-month performance, the player will usually show incremental improvement, and being compared to better players will not discourage them. Can you use CBE with your team?

If your team does fall short of the forecast, what should you do? May I suggest you take a realistic assessment of where they fell short? *The first place to look is in the mirror.* Were your guidance and leadership what you would expect of a winning leader? When I was a teenager, Paul Bryant was head coach at Alabama, and Ralph Jordan was head coach at Auburn. It puzzled me why when these teams won, their head coaches heaped praise upon the players, their effort, and the assistant coaches for game management and for preparing great game plans. When they lost, these same head coaches would take the blame themselves for making mistakes in game management or not having prepared the team properly. As an adult, I learned from Dave Anderson that *"the speed of the leader was the speed of the pack"* and that *"a fish rots from the head down . . . not from the tail up!"* I realized then why Coach Bryant and Coach Jordan reacted the way they did when their team lost. The first place to look when the team does not measure up is at the coach.

Then I learned to go back to the TASTE model and look at myself through that prism. After all, I am the coach, and they are the players.

1. Did I provide the <u>Truth</u> about our performance during the month so they could change direction?
2. Did I hold myself and the team members <u>Accountable</u> for using the processes and systems we had in place?
3. Was I providing an adequate level of <u>Support</u> to ensure that they had the proper tools and enough information to perform at the expected level?

4. Did I show <u>Trust</u> that the team could do what was expected based on the directions they received from me?

5. Was my team <u>Empowered</u> to perform up to their potential, or did I stifle their creativity and discourage their initiative?

In almost every case when we did not perform well, I found an issue with myself. Then I corrected the issue. Once the issue was resolved, the problem disappeared.

In addition to examining myself, I found it beneficial to go back to the 4 Ps: People, Process, Product, and Promotion. These must be managed for the team to perform at a high level. They need to be examined in the proper order to determine what to improve so that the team can succeed. Always start by examining the People— that is where most problems begin and end.

Start with <u>PEOPLE</u>:

1. Are they properly trained to do the job?
2. Do they have the tools to do the job?
3. Are they properly organized to accomplish the goals in the forecast?
4. Do we have the right people in the right jobs?
5. Do we have enough people to do the job?
6. Are the individuals on the team motivated to do what is required to win?
7. Do we have people with negative attitudes? Why?

If we seem to have the right people and we are satisfied that we do not have people problems, then we move on to <u>PROCESS</u>. Great people saddled with sub-par processes will not support your efforts to build a winning team.

1. What process or processes are hindering us from succeeding?
2. Are our processes aligned with the Best Practices of others providing the same products or services? How do we compare with our own best efforts?
3. Has the team bought into our processes because we displayed how those processes aid in our effort to succeed?
4. Do the team members have ideas about how to improve our processes? If so, what are their suggestions?
5. Is there new technology that will allow us to change our processes making us substantially better at what we do?
6. Are our processes designed and aligned to meet or exceed what our clients expect?

Here we need to pause. If our problems do not lie with the coach and we have the right people and our processes are aligned for success, then should we examine our products and services to set the team on the right path?

Next, let's examine our <u>PRODUCT</u>:

1. Is there still a market for the product or service that we are offering?
2. Is there an upsell product or service that we can offer to

pump up sales?

3. In examining the questions that we receive through websites, do they provide a clue to a product or service issue?

4. Do our reviews indicate an issue with our product or service?

5. Has the technology associated with the product or service become obsolete?

6. Has a competitor introduced a product or service that our clients want more than what we are selling?

Question #6 is important. Many companies have had to either bring a new product to market or reinvent themselves to succeed. When Burger King introduced the Whopper, they succeeded in attracting many clients away from McDonald's. When McDonald's countered back with the Big Mac, they regained their market dominance and never looked back. Amazon began first as an online used book store. They declined rapidly when Barnes & Noble and Books-A-Million cut into their book sales. So, Amazon reinvented itself as an online store selling almost anything that you could possibly want. And because they own their warehouses and their delivery vehicles, they set the gold standard in allowing clients to shop from home and get quick free delivery.

The last place to look at is <u>PROMOTION</u>. Many leaders look at their marketing and messaging first to determine what is keeping them from success. That is the wrong approach because their real problem is usually with people or processes. Look at marketing last after you examine the other issues.

Let's examine why marketing may be the problem.

1. Are your marketing messages in alignment with the same message online, on-air, in print, and in-store? This is the #1 reason why your marketing may be ineffective. Remember that effective marketing has the prospect experiencing your message at least 3 times.

2. Is your messaging believable? If not, your team members will not believe it and neither will your prospects.

3. Are you online? Online targeted ads on your website, Google, Facebook, Amazon, affiliates, and your email campaigns provide you with the greatest exposure for your message at the least expense.

4. Is your online marketing structured for cell phone screens? Over 70% of all shoppers start their search on their cell phones or tablets.

5. If using electronic media, television, or radio, are you buying enough spots for your prospective audience to hear your same message at least 3 times? If not, you do not have enough frequency.

6. Is your electronic advertising timed to be delivered when your prospects are in their cars(radio) or watching TV? If not, you are buying the wrong times.

7. Are you targeting your primary audience or scattering your shot hoping to hit everybody?

8. If using billboards, is your message readable for at least 7 seconds? If not, change locations. Does your message utilize 7 words or less? If not, it is too wordy.

We have covered a lot of territory in this section. At this point, let me reiterate that if you are not achieving your forecast, look first at yourself, then your team, and then your processes. You will find that 95 out of 100 issues will be uncovered in one of those areas.

SECTION FIVE:

TEAM BUILDING

CHAPTER 18: THE 4 STAGES OF TEAM MEMBER DEVELOPMENT

You added 2 highly qualified people to your team of 15 just 2 months ago. They have great credentials, aced their initial zoom interviews, and really impressed all during their in-person interviews. The current team members were happy to have these new members to help them clear out the backlog of work. These top performers hit the ground running, and it looked like you hit two back-to-back home runs. Now, however, there is growing friction within the team. One of these new hires is very upset with two other team members. The other new person is on the verge of resigning because she feels that the rest of the team does not respect her. You are ready to pull out your hair and are losing sleep with the team unrest. What caused these issues and what should you do to correct them?

To formulate a plan to address this friction, we need to back up and understand the 4 stages of team member development. Most teams will experience the effects of these 4 stages. Understanding what they are and how they affect both individual and team performance is key to preventing these issues and addressing them if they appear in your team.

These 4 stages of team member development are as follows:

- Stage 1: Forming
- Stage 2: Storming
- Stage 3: Norming
- Stage 4: Performing

Let's examine each stage separately and then put them back together to see how they affect the team in real life.

STAGE 1: FORMING—the new team member just started

- Enthusiasm is high
- Skill level is low

They have a basic understanding of what they will be doing; however, they need to learn your products and services plus your processes. Their enthusiasm is off the charts high, and they cannot wait to get started. This enthusiasm helps them to overcome challenges initially even though they have a lot to learn and will possibly make many mistakes. In this initial stage, the team member's performance may well be above average. The other team members are excited about having the new person. This is the honeymoon period.

STAGE 2: STORMING—the new is wearing off

- Enthusiasm is low
- Skill level is low

This is the dangerous stage and usually occurs about 60 – 90 days after they start with the new team. The job is more complex or difficult than they originally thought. They have made several mistakes. Some of their coworkers possibly are not happy about continuing to show the new person what to do or how to do it. There can be clashes of personalities based on the new person's expectations and the current team members' expectations. If the team is not properly coached during this period, the leader did not do a good job explaining that what they are experiencing is a normal step in the evolution of a new team member. During this storming period, your team members will need more of your support. The new person needs support because their enthusiasm is lower—usually because they are still not entirely comfortable in the new job. The other team members need your support to understand that these conflicts are normal. Plus, they need to rally around to help the new member perform up to expectations. If your new person is going to leave the team, it usually occurs between 60 – 120 days of their start date.

STAGE 3: NORMING—things are starting to get better, and the conflicts subside

- Enthusiasm is average or slightly above average
- Skill level is average or slightly above average

The new team member has progressed to where they are comfortable with their role and has achieved competency in their job. The other team members discovered what the new person is capable of doing. Plus, they have a degree of confidence that the new person will be there for the long term. Fewer clashes between teammates occur, so tasks get done correctly and on time. In short, the team has achieved some normalcy due to the skills and cooperation of all team members. This stage, Norming, is the stage in which most teams will remain until another personnel change occurs. They will have some brilliance and some issues. Overall, the team will perform well and get their tasks completed.

STAGE 4: PERFORMING—above-average performance is now the standard

- Enthusiasm is high
- Skill Level is high

This is the sweet spot where excellence is the standard. Now all the team members, including the new person, have combined their efforts and skills to achieve great things together. They outperform competitors. They win championships. They set a high standard and dare anyone to challenge them. These team members all love each other and pull together to help whenever any team member has an issue, whether personal or professional. This is where every leader wants their team to be. Fewer than 5% of teams ever make it to Stage 4.

Let's now take the time to identify how to expand your knowledge of the 4 stages of team member development to avoid situations like the scenario we just discussed. We will analyze each stage individually.

STAGE 1: FORMING

We will break this stage into 3 sections: Recruiting, Interviewing, and Selection.

Recruiting is a constant exercise. To get the best prospects, you must always be looking for individuals who match the skills and attitude that you want on your team. Start with a thorough job description. You must know <u>what</u> you need to know <u>who</u> you need. Be sure to include in the job description, core competencies, special skills or education, and preferred experience as well as the tasks a team member must complete. Remember to *Hire for Attitude, Train for Skills!* A candidate may not have the skills required yet. However, with the right attitude, they may be able to learn the necessary skills.

Next, if this has not already been done, get the personality evaluations on your current team members. Look for people with similar personality traits as your top performers. The odds are if you can get a candidate with similar personality traits to these top performers, you have a good chance of getting someone who can be a top performer. If you have a position to fill that requires a personality not displayed by any other member of the current team, then you will also know more about what to look for.

Many online avenues are available to recruit new team members. You can use pre-screening services like Indeed and Zip-Recruiter, trade-specific newspapers for your industry such as Automotive News and Restaurant News, placement firms like Robert Half, Facebook groups, LinkedIn groups . . . this list is endless. In addition to sites online, here are some other unconventional ways to recruit:

- You need team members with great people skills. You interact with a cashier at your local grocery store or drug store; a talented manager or server at your favorite restaurant, coffee, or bagel shop; or possibly a delivery person with a great personality.

- You have associations with numerous prospective team members through your church, service club or organization, union, or local business group. Be attentive to members who may be a good fit for your team.

- You offer a graduated bonus to any team member who refers a prospective team member who you hire: $200 if they stay for 90 days, another $300 if they stay for 6 months, and another $400 if remain employed for a year.

- You have clients with employees that have skills you want for your team. Be careful with this one, as you may lose a good client if you hire away their star performer(s).

- Additionally, in larger organizations, there may be team members ready to promote or get transferred that you can get using your company's HR internal hiring process. This is especially true if the company or organization has locations in different areas and where a team member's spouse is being transferred into your area and they want to stay with the organization when they relocate.

Interviewing the prospect is the next step in the selection process. You have reviewed their résumé and supporting documents and are ready to proceed. I recommend the following process:

1. Start with an unscheduled phone call if possible. When you call someone, they will not be prepared for an interaction. Thus, if you get a chance to speak with them, you will hear how they sound unfiltered. This call is to introduce yourself and your company and to find out more about what the prospect is seeking. If the prospect does not have good phone manners, they will probably not have good manners in person. This phone call is a screening process. Let your prospect do most of the talking. If the call is good, you can either schedule an in-person interview, schedule a video interview, or share with them that you have numerous candidates to contact and you will re-contact by a certain date.

2. Assuming that you have promised a recontact by a certain date, ensure that you call, text, or email them as you said you would. You represent your team and you need to keep your word. In the interim between your initial call and your follow-up call or interview, be attentive to any recontact from the candidate to you. This can be a good indication of the level of professionalism of this person.

If no contact between these sessions occurs, that does not necessarily mean they are not qualified; good phone skills can be taught. Having a recontact from the candidate for either an appointment confirmation or a thank you for being considered gives you an indication of how the prospect will interact with your other team members and with your clients.

3. If you cannot reach them via phone, email or text them to let them know of your interest to talk via phone. If no response, go on to the next candidate. If you reach them via email or text then schedule a phone call (see #1).

4. If you have the availability of a personality evaluation, it would be best if you have the candidate complete one before the second meeting. This information will give you some insights into the way the person views themselves and may indicate if they are experiencing some major stress currently. Either way, you will simply have more insight into the real person before your second discussion.

5. For your interview, set up enough time for a thorough discussion. Be sure to have a standard set of questions that cannot be answered *"Yes"* or *"No."* You want to utilize open-ended questions that require detailed answers from them. These questions should be used with every candidate to prevent an opportunity for someone to claim discrimination or bias later. If you do not get a thorough or understandable answer to a question, ask follow-up questions. Also, understand that the person who asks questions has control. Invest your time asking questions, not making

statements. Here are some possible interview questions designed to draw out the candidate so you can see the real person, not just the candidate who has been coached and has practiced answers to basic standard questions.

    a.   *"Please share why you are leaving (or have left) your current job."*

    b.   *"Please describe the relationship you have with your coworkers." "With your boss?" "Why do you say that?"*

    c.   *"Please describe what a normal workday is like in your current (or former) position." "How do you feel about that?"*

    d.   *"Please describe in detail the biggest win or triumph that you have had in your life so far." "How about at work or on the job?"*

    e.   *"Please describe in detail the best day you ever had in any job. What was the outcome for you?"*

    f.   *"What was the biggest mistake you ever made at work? What happened? What was the outcome for you based on that event?"*

    g.   *"What training do you feel you need to progress in your career?" "Why?"*

    h.   *"What do you expect from a boss or team leader?" "Why do you feel that way?"*

6. The interview will end in one of several ways (be sure to follow the HR protocols for interviewing and hiring for your organization):

    a. Either of you will terminate the interview and there will be no follow-up scheduled.

    b. The interview concludes with a statement about your consideration of other applicants and you will be inviting the top interviewees for further action.

    c. The interview concludes with a follow-up session (electronic or in person) either with yourself or another company official.

    d. The offer of employment based on a background check.

7. <u>Very important..."*Hire for Attitude...Train for Skills.*"</u>

8. Be sure that ALL new hires sign a statement that they are entering a 60-day probationary period where either party, for any reason, may terminate their employment. We will see why in the STORMING stage later.

9. Once the decision has been made to hire a new team member, seal the deal!

    a. Contact them first with a personal phone call from you.

    b. Send confirmation emails and texts.

    c. Let your team members know of the hire as soon as possible.

    d. Send them something of value to their home address so that they will be certain that they made the best decision for themselves by joining your team:

      i. This can be a company hat, tee-shirt, coffee cup, insulated water bottle, or even a small flower arrangement.

      ii. A short hand-written *"Welcome"* card or note is special.

   e. If you have ever hired someone and they did not show up for their 1st day, you understand why this last touch is designed to *"Seal The Deal!"*

On their 1st day, introduce the new member to their coworkers. If you have done your job, they will be expecting the new hire. If they will have a particular workstation, have that area cleaned and ready for them (you probably sent them a text with a picture of their work area and a statement that "we have prepared your new place for you"). Take them on a quick tour so they know where the bathroom, break room, and related areas are located. If a trip to HR to complete paperwork is in order, escort them to HR and introduce them. Have this 1st day set up to be memorable. Then get them either working or in training as soon as possible.

Just as their 1st day is important, the next 60 days will determine the length and severity of STAGE 2, Storming. You should be able to determine in the first 3 weeks if the new hire is a good fit for your team. If not, take action. Remember that they agreed to a 60-day probationary period when they came onboard. Use it quickly if you discover that you made a mistake. Remember the old adage: *"Hire Slow and Fire Fast."*

STAGE 2: STORMING

If you followed the process outlined in Stage 1, Forming, you will have fewer problems during this sophomore term for the new team member. There will be issues that crop up that need to be addressed quickly. Handle them quickly; issues that are ignored metastasize like cancers and infect your team—even your entire organization.

Conflicts may arise for many reasons. Getting the 2 team members together, away from the other team members, to talk things out settles many conflicts quickly. This encourages both of them to be adults and work out their differences on their own. This action by you to get them together away from you and everyone else sends a clear message to the rest of the team that you will not be the group sheriff and get involved in every little issue that appears. It also shows that you care enough to set them up for success and that you trust them to be accountable for their actions. However, if they cannot work out their differences and you must get involved, put them in a room with you and use this process.

1. State emphatically that you expect every team member to be an adult and to first try to handle the issue themselves.
2. Get them to acknowledge their inability to work out the issue between them.
3. Let them know that since they have involved you, you will make the decision for all to abide by and they will follow the process you have for this issue. Also, firmly state that neither will probably leave the meeting completely satisfied.

4. Have one speak at a time and instruct the other to be completely quiet. If you need further clarification, ask that person a question. Do not allow any interruptions.

5. When the first person is finished, instruct that person to be completely quiet. Have the other person now speak to the problem with no interruptions. If you have questions, ask them directly.

6. Make your decision and let them both know that the decision is final. Before dismissing them, restate that you do not appreciate them causing a problem that affects the rest of the team and your decision is final and ends the discussion.

7. You need to understand that this process will temporarily make you the "Bad Guy" to both of them. That is a good thing in that they will, at last, have something they can agree on. They will come to respect you more and the rest of the team will appreciate the reduced level of bad feelings.

Most every team leader or coach would like to have a group of superstars on their team. This perceived blessing can be a problem initially. A *Top Performer* usually has a big ego. They want to be seen as <u>the</u> *Top Performer*, and they have a strong desire to win in every encounter. Having 2 or more team members with the same mindset and strong personality will many times create friction between them, which sometimes plays out in front of the rest of the team. As their coach, emphasizing the importance of everyone working together to achieve the team's goals and acknowledging how important their contributions are to the success of the team, which feeds their egos, is important for the team. If these two team members' egos are causing a problem, then refer to the process in the previous paragraph.

Now let's return to the scenario that opened this chapter. Sounds like this team is in Stage 2: STORMING. As noted, this is a dangerous stage to be in. Many qualified team members, both new and those who have short tenures, leave a team because issues like this are not resolved. Let's use Dale Carnegie's method for problem-solving by answering these 4 questions:

1. Clearly describe the problem?
2. What has caused the problem?
3. What are the possible options?
4. Which option do you recommend?

We do not have enough information to answer question #1. We obviously have some team members who are having difficulty getting along. But, is that the real problem or just window dressing on a deeper issue. It could be a competence issue. It most likely includes some trust issues. It may be a clash of personalities between well-qualified team members. You will not know until you can answer question #1.

Bear in mind that when you ask each individual privately, *"What is the problem?"* you may not get the real answer. One method for getting the information you need is to ask this follow-up question. *"In addition to what you just told me, what else is a problem for you?"* Most people when asked a difficult question will tell what they assume you want to hear with the first question. By asking this follow-up question you will very likely hear the real issue.

When you are sure that the person has genuinely answered the 1st question, or answered more clearly with the follow-up question, then ask question #2: *"What exactly caused the problem?"* The next follow-up question will be, *"Is there something else that could have caused the problem?"* You are now getting a better picture of the circumstances causing the problem.

When the team member answers question #3: *"What are the possible solutions to the problem?"* they may display a lot of emotion and have only one answer. Always require an alternate solution. If you get more than one solution you can move on to question #4: *"Which solution do you recommend?"*

Use that line of questioning with each team member individually. Take notes. Then, before concluding the interview, ask them if they have anything to add. Sometimes that last question will open the floodgates of information and emotion, especially concerning their feelings. Just listen and take notes. After your discussion, let them know that you appreciate them as a person and that all team members will be interviewed, so the team can mend and move forward.

After your interviews with all team members individually, make your decision about any personnel changes. If termination is required, do it quickly, and in private. Then let the rest of the team know what happened. Share with them how this could have been avoided and assign most of the blame to yourself.

If no personnel changes are required, share with the entire team what you have discovered in answer to the 4 questions. Announce any task assignment or process changes to solve the problem and close the meeting. This professional process for conflict resolution is quite helpful in restoring the team synergy and cooperation required to move from Storming to Norming.

Let's pause our discussion now for 2 questions:
How would you have handled that situation differently?

- _______________________________________
- _______________________________________
- _______________________________________

What result do you expect to get by the way you handled it?

- _______________________________________
- _______________________________________
- _______________________________________

Before we leave STAGE 2 in team member development, we need to acknowledge that there is always a chance of your team falling into this area of conflict whenever a new team member arrives. How well you do in STAGE 1 at the beginning, and how adept you are at dealing with people issues will determine how often you enter STAGE 2 and how long you remain there.

STAGE 3: NORMING

As you enter this NORMING stage in team member development you will notice an improvement in the skill level of all team members. With better performance increased by their improving skill levels, the individual team members' enthusiasm for the functions and goals of the team will grow. Now is the time when your coaching skills will be required. Keep the team members focused on the goals of the team. continue to train and retrain them, introducing updated tools and systems. When team members celebrate winning performances (individual and group milestones), they will experience more efficiency and improved productivity, increasing team spirit. Keep them focused by not allowing backsliding and by celebrating every win. NORMING is a good place for your team to reside. In fact, this is where most teams will operate consistently. The question is: *"Is this as far as you want to go?"*

STAGE 4: PERFORMING

Jim Collins, in his book, *Good to Great*, examines the differences between teams that consistently operate as good teams and those that achieve championship team status. The top-performing, consistently winning, high-performance teams seem to operate at a level above everyone else.

How many times have we seen a new leader or coach come in and raise the team to championship level? Take a moment now and list some leaders or coaches that created teams, organizations, businesses—even states and countries—to a championship level:

- ____
- ____

Now ask yourself, how did they do it? Was it just luck? Did the circumstances just fall into place and they took advantage of them? Was there some special *"it"* factor that they had to propel their teams, organizations, businesses, or governments to the top?

Take a moment now and list several things you think aided the leaders you listed earlier to their championship levels:

- ____
- ____
- ____

Let's take a look at the traits of some Championship Leaders . . . .

__Great leaders set very high goals and always demand the best from themselves and the people on their teams.__

Lincoln knew that the cause to end slavery and save the Union from being broken apart was justified. He demanded the best from the leaders of the Union army. He kept replacing generals until he found and promoted Ulysses Grant. Together they won the American Civil War and saved the nation.

He was focused on ending the scourge of slavery and kept everyone around him focused as well. Lincoln knew that winning the war would not be enough to end slavery. Thus, he used the art of persuasion, plus every political and economic tool available to him to push through the 13th Amendment to the Constitution to end slavery forever in all the states and territories of the US.

Great leaders create a culture of winning that does not accept nor allow setbacks and difficulties to derail their pursuit of excellence. They have a shared vision that all their team members see and buy into.

Walt Disney was told that building a business around a cartoon mouse was foolish and would bankrupt him. Working with his team, they not only created Mickey Mouse, but his team also built a brand that has endured for over 90 years. Then he built a theme park in California around all of the characters, which has been delighting guests for over 65 years. In addition, Disney is one of the most recognized and enduring brands on the globe.

The smart financial experts thought Walt Disney had lost his mind when he bought 27,000 acres of swampland in central Florida outside the then small town of Orlando. Note that the Disney World theme park celebrated its 50th anniversary in 2021, welcoming and entertaining millions of guests every year. Businesses from all over the world have studied the business and culture at Disney World to learn how success follows a fierce dedication to excellence and customer-centric service.

__Great leaders know that their success depends on developing the players on their teams to their fullest potential. They have a process that builds on their previous success of creating strong talented players who will continue their tradition of winning.__

Nick Saban was a talented, winning coach who won a National Championship at LSU. He accepted the challenge of turning around the football program at Alabama even though he could have continued his winning ways at LSU until retirement. In leading the program at Alabama, he has won 6 more national championships and along the way has become the standard against whom other coaches are measured.

Saban's Alabama teams have adopted the attitude of *"Next Man Up."* This business like approach by his players means that everyone on the team practices as though they will start the next game. If a player goes down due to injury or other issues the next player knows he has to perform to a high standard because he is the *Next Man Up.* Every year, Alabama competes at the highest level because of the deep bench of available players developed under Coach Saban's winning program.

<u>Great leaders pull together other talented, competing leaders, organize them effectively, and use their strengths to achieve complicated, seemingly unreachable goals.</u>

General Dwight Eisenhower was placed in charge of other leaders who had been his superior officers earlier in his career. Additionally, he was tasked to build a successful coalition of armies from Great Britain, Canada, France, and the US along with freedom fighters from all over Europe to defeat the German and Italian forces. Because of his leadership, this unruly group of leaders with competing interests defeated the Axis powers and ended WWII in Europe in 3 ½ years.

As president in the 1950s, he used those same leadership skills to help in the rebuilding of post-war Europe, stand up to the military advances of the communist Soviet Union, and bring about one of the strongest economic expansions in US history.

This next task is very important to the development of your winning team. Dwell on these questions—then answer them so you can put your own success plan together.

1. What are the traits that you will absolutely require to be present in the team members that you coach?
2. Who will you mentor to help you build a consistently winning organization?
3. How will having a deep bench of *Next Person Up* allow your team to grow?
4. How will you manage the 4 Ps that will help to guide your team to achieve their goals?
5. When will you start this process?
6. When will you achieve your first milestone or benchmark?

CHAPTER 19: EFFECTIVE MEETINGS

Before we discuss all the attributes of an effective meeting, I want you to write this phrase on a sticky note or index card and put it on your computer, your refrigerator at home, and on the mirror where you shave or put on your make-up:

LIFE REWARDS ACTION!

You can read, you can investigate, you can think, you can research, and you can plan. All those verbs are central to building high-performing teams and having effective meetings. However, none of those functions by themselves will bring about success. Only by taking <u>ACTION</u> will you move your team forward, have success, and achieve your goals.

Creating or inciting <u>ACTION</u> is the only legitimate purpose of a meeting. You can teach, present, discuss, poll, motivate, create emotion, energize, and inform in a meeting. However, all successful meetings create <u>ACTION</u>. As we discuss all things about meetings, keep the requirement of creating <u>ACTION</u> foremost in your mind. Let's continue.

My first meeting as a rookie automobile salesman in 1980 went like this. I was told to be in the conference room at 8:30 a.m. sharp! Not wanting to be late, I was in the room at 8:15 a.m . . . by myself. At 8:29, several other experienced salespersons showed up for this meeting. By 8:35, the rest of the sales team was in the room, complaining about having to be in so early, or talking about sports, cars, etc. At 8:37, one of the sales managers arrived and asked where the other sales manager was. At 8:39, the other sales manager arrived stating he had been stuck in traffic. That is when the meeting commenced.

During this mandatory session, we were informed that there were several vehicles left unlocked and not parked in their appropriate spaces the night before at closing time. We were reprimanded for only selling one car yesterday and currently being short of our sales goal by 15 units. We were directed to get off our butts and start doing our jobs or else. The only positive thing we heard was from one of the salespeople who thanked another salesperson for assisting him by selling his customer last night. That created another firestorm of managerial instruction berating the salesperson who was not there to take care of his customer last night. He was warned to be sure to have someone informed and available in the event of his absence next time or he would lose his commission on the sale. This "depression session" ended at 9:20 a.m. with no one in the mood to sell a car. I wondered quietly what I had gotten myself into by coming to work there.

We discussed the need to create action within our meetings. What action do you think was created by the meeting I just described? We will revisit this meeting a little later in this chapter.

Every successful meeting must have a stated purpose, which leads to some form of action. When Eisenhower met with his commanders on June 5, 1944, the day before the D-day invasion of Europe, the purpose was to decide whether they would execute the landings on June 6th or 7th. The decision was made to schedule the D-day landings on June 6, 1944. When I met with my future father-in-law at a restaurant in Oxford, Alabama in 1970, the purpose was to ask for his blessing so I could marry his daughter. We were married 6 months later. Understanding that the purpose of a meeting is to create some action. Did both of those meetings meet that standard?

There are different types of meetings. There are scheduled, planned meetings and those that are not planned but occur due to circumstances or unforeseen opportunities. There are training and informational meetings that can be group meetings or one-on-one coaching. There are meetings to report on statuses, results, and outcomes. There are collaborative sessions, conferences, and conventions with large and diverse groups. There are meetings held in person or online. Regardless of size, location, who is involved, or the timing of the meeting, there must be a facilitator and a purpose that involves action. Let's discuss the role of the facilitator.

The facilitator may plan the meeting or simply control a meeting that someone else has planned. For example, a teacher may use their lesson plan or a lesson plan someone else provided. An editor who holds a staff meeting every Monday at 9:00 a.m. may use their agenda or one prepared by their assistant. Regardless of who is facilitating the meeting or producing the agenda, every planned meeting should have a written agenda.

A written agenda circulated prior to the start of the meeting accomplishes several important tasks. The agenda alerts attendees to the planned discussions for the session and prompts them to gather the necessary materials needed to address issues and answer inquiries, have backup data to defend their positions, and provide needed documentation allowing the group to form and commit to action plans. It helps keep the group's discussion focused, allowing the facilitator to keep the meeting moving in the recommended direction in a timely manner. Most meetings without a written agenda skip vital information, have discussions that are not focused or productive, and, worst of all, do not conclude with an action plan or plans. Additionally, not having an agenda disrespects the time and talents of the attendees.

Here is a sample sales meeting agenda:

Sales Meeting Agenda: Monday, January 30, 2022, 8:30 a.m.

Location: conference room on 2nd floor

A) Success stories by sales consultants:
   a. Bob @ Burgess family
   b. Sally @ 2 trade-ins from Stephens family
B) New Vehicle Report from new vehicle sales manager:
   a. Update on incoming inventory and sold units
   b. Incentive enhancements
   c. New process of new vehicle predelivery inspection
C) Used Vehicle Report from used vehicle sales manager:
   a. Review recent purchased vehicles and trade-ins lined up in front of building
   b. Return to conference room
   c. Lot vehicles scheduled to be cleaned Wednesday,

2/2/22 morning

D) Role-play training:

    a. Bob and Sally handling a trade-in objection

    b. Laura and Frank handling a payment objection

E) Salesperson commitment to process improvement

F) Showroom car walk-around presentation by Horace

    a. _______________________________________

    b. _______________________________________

    c. _______________________________________

G) Q & A

This agenda was emailed to all attendees on Friday afternoon, 1/28/22. Any manager in the sales department may facilitate this meeting agenda. All recipients know that they are required to participate. The agenda shows respect for the attendees and assigns responsibilities for various individuals to be ready for their part in having a successful session:

- Facilitator: starts meeting on a positive note with 2 success stories
- New vehicle sales manager: provides information on incoming stock and sold vehicles, changes in factor incentives, and a new PDI process
- Used vehicle sales manager: has newly arrived used vehicles in line at front of building for salespeople to preview and announces the lot clean up schedule
- Bob and Sally: responsible for demonstrating trade-in objection handling
- Laura and Frank: responsible for demonstrating payment objection handling

- Each salesperson: commit to their sales quota for the week
- Horace: responsible for a simulated vehicle presentation in the showroom
- Facilitator: handles Q&A and closes session in the showroom

Note the action items:

- Session opens with success stories putting all in a positive frame of mind.
- Sales managers are responsible for their action items in their section.
- Salespeople are responsible for using the information to sell more units.
- All salespersons win by learning and relearning closing techniques.
- Salespeople commit to the necessary actions to meet their individual quotas.
- All salespersons win by learning or relearning the proper walk-around process.
- Session ends in the showroom on a positive note with all attendees ready for action.

Take just a moment now and compare the meeting plan and agenda above with the first sales meeting I attended in 1980. Which meeting would you rather attend?

Now let's discuss one-on-one coaching sessions. Use a standard written coaching plan so the person who is being coached knows how the session will be handled and what they need to bring to the session. A sample standard sales one-on-one coaching plan may look like this.

- The salesperson brings their written sales quota commitment to include what part of the process they will work to improve this week.
- The manager reviews the performance data with the salesperson so both can see progress being made or if a correction is required.
- They review together the list of hot prospects that the salesperson is working on to set up a plan to get them closed.
- Salesperson requests help in whatever area they need, including having the manager contact a prospect to help close the deal.
- Both commit to working together so the salesperson's skill level will improve.

One-on-one coaching sessions are the best way to train someone because the training is specially designed to help the individual improve. Planning sessions for your people scheduled at regular intervals are best. That way very little will slip through the cracks because both parties are accountable for the success of the team member. They keep the team member's progress on track. Plus, these sessions help you grow your bench faster than with group meetings.

Here are a few more notes on handling successful meetings:
Start and end the meetings on time. This shows your professional-

ism and your respect for the time of the attendees.

Be sure your agenda states the purpose of the meeting. The facilitator should reiterate the purpose, briefly, so all attendees know what is expected.

The facilitator must keep the discussion on track, referring back to the agenda or the purpose of the meeting if necessary.

Use Dale Carnegie's 4 imperatives to promote productive discussion. These will make the participants accountable and not allow the meeting to dissolve into a complaint session.

Problems or suggestions must be put in front of the group using this format:

1. Clearly state the problem or opportunity so all will understand what you are discussing.
2. Clearly share what has caused this problem or opportunity.
3. Share with the group the options you see that are available to either solve the problem or take advantage of the opportunity.
4. Share with the group which option you recommend and why you recommend it.

When decisions are made, the facilitator should announce them clearly and state who is accountable for the execution and follow-up of the actions required by the decision. For discussions tabled during the meeting, assign the responsible parties who will work together to solve the problem or take advantage of the opportunity. Be sure to set a time limit for the person or group to report back, so those who are assigned the issue will address and solve it promptly.

At the end of the session, there should be a quick summary of what was accomplished and what further actions are required, so there will be no confusion about who is responsible. Maintain a written and/or recorded review of the session for follow-up and accountability.

Now it is time for you to create a meeting agenda for your next meeting using these notes and this process. Then commit to using a written agenda with every planned meeting or training session.

SECTION SIX:
CONCLUSION AND REVIEW

CHAPTER 20: UNLEASHING YOUR INNER COACH

To unleash your inner coach, we must first define and then understand what a coach really is:

A coach is a <u>leader</u>. That does not necessarily mean that a leader is the "Boss." In my career, I have had the opportunity to <u>coach up</u> to managers or owners who ranked above me in the organization. Many felt that for an idea or program to be effective it must be their idea. For me, as a leader, when an idea needed action or a program needed to be implemented, my job was to make the person above me think it was their idea or program so that we would be assured of their complete support. I have had the opportunity to <u>coach sideways</u> with managers in the same position as me so they would learn from me, understand our mission, and support our team, assuring our collaborative efforts would succeed. I invested most of my time <u>coaching down</u> to assist team members in developing their full potential and growing our bench of future leaders, allowing the organization the opportunity to grow and succeed.

A coach is a <u>mentor</u>. The mentor is someone who embodies the qualities they are endeavoring to instill in the people they lead. If the mentor sets a bad example in their personal life, they lose the respect of the team and the ability to be effective as a leader. When the mentor lives the life that they want the team members to have, being a great example of what they can be, they inspire others, and their leadership is both justified and effective.

A coach is an <u>organizer</u>. The organizer sees all the steps and short-term achievements required for the team to achieve its goals. The organizer puts people, equipment, processes, and structure in place so the team can be successful in completing the steps to achieve their ultimate goals.

A coach is an <u>instigator</u>. The instigator makes things happen. When the team gets stuck or needs a course correction, the instigator rearranges people, tools, and events or changes course to get the team back on track to achieve their goals.

A coach is a <u>disciplinarian</u>. As a disciplinarian, the coach must administer fair and personal consequences for those who willfully cause the team to veer away from required processes, violate team ethics, or cause harm to another team player. When administering the requisite punishment for these violations, the coach is not only helping the violator to get back on a successful path, but is also signaling to the rest of the team the importance of always doing the right thing.

A coach is a <u>cheerleader</u>. As a cheerleader, the coach provides the needed personal and professional support to any team member. The coach applauds successes and helps team members up after a loss. The coach also helps the rest of the team celebrate both individual and team wins and accomplishments.

Most importantly, the coach is a <u>teacher</u>. The teacher-coach realizes that they must be the person who first and foremost instructs the team as a group and members as individuals on how to improve skills, efforts, and attitudes to achieve successful outcomes. To achieve maximum success, you must be all the persons described above:

- Leader
- Mentor
- Organizer
- Instigator
- Disciplinarian
- Cheerleader
- Teacher

You will also need to utilize this basic process known by every successful teacher:

1. _Tell them what you will be telling them;_ this sets the stage to begin instruction by sharing with the learners what to

expect and what will be covered.

2. *Tell them what you said you would tell them;* deliver the information that you promised in step one—you created that expectation, so now deliver on it.

3. *Tell them what you told them;* review the key points in your presentation to make them stick.

This sounds crazy, even redundant. You may even say that you told them what to expect and they should be paying attention, even taking notes. What you need to understand is that for information to be remembered, the person whom you are teaching must be exposed to it 3 times. That is a basic rule in teaching. People need to be exposed to the information at least 3 times to remember it. That also applies in advertising: tell them what you will be telling them; tell them; then tell them what you told them. That process follows the 3-times rule. If only one message exists in an ad, then to be effective, the listener or viewer must see or hear it 3 times. However, if the ad states the message 3-times, then the person to whom the ad is directed can remember it, making it a much more effective ad.

It is now time for you to unleash your inner coach. What changes will you commit to yourself in order to unleash the exceptional leader in you?

REVIEW

SECTION ONE: THE NEED FOR DYNAMIC LEADERSHIP

- Defining Leadership
- TASTE Model

  - Truth
  - Accountability
  - Support
  - Trust
  - Empowerment

- Leadership stories
- Creating and communicating *"VISION"*
- Leadership vs. Management

SECTION TWO: FORECASTING

- The Need for Forecasting and Benchmarking
- Gathering Data for your Forecast
- Time Sensitive Forecasting
- Communicating Your Forecast

SECTION THREE: LEADERSHIP DISCIPLINES; THE 4 Ps

- People
- Processes and Systems
- Products and Services
- Promotion

SECTION FOUR: ACTION PLAN STEPS

- Step 1: Forecast an Average Month
- Step 2: Establish Your People Action Plan
- Step 3: Establish Your Process and Systems Action Plan
- Step 4: Establish Your Products and Services Action Plan
- Step 5: Establish Your Promotional Action Plan
- Step 6: Review and Adjust Your Action Plans

SECTION FIVE: TEAM BUILDING

- 4 Stages of Team Member Development

  - Forming
  - Storming
  - Norming
  - Performing
  - Growing Your Bench

- Effective Meetings

SECTION SIX: CONCLUSION AND REVIEW

- Unleashing Your Inner Coach
- Leader
- Mentor
- Organizer
- Instigator
- Disciplinarian
- Cheerleader
- Teacher

  o 3 Elements of Effective Teaching

ACKNOWLEDGMENTS

With reverence and sincere appreciation, I humbly acknowledge the inspiration and guidance of our Holy Father, our Savior Jesus Christ, and the Holy Spirit. They lead me in my actions, my relationships, and my efforts. I am very much in debt to them.

In 1994, as a new general manager of an automobile dealership in Savannah, Georgia, I had the privilege of being exposed to this highly effective and very successful method of organizational leadership. By studying, utilizing, and mastering these 4 Ps, the teams which I have been privileged to lead successfully moved from underperforming to achieving goals that many thought were not possible. Guiding other leaders, teaching the process, setting a proper example, and mentoring these leaders in business, churches, and service organizations have allowed me to "pay it forward," so others may enjoy the success they have worked hard to achieve. They are now mentoring others and training many more future leaders. It would be impossible for me to proceed without paying tribute to the many individuals who came before me and had a positive, enriching, and informative effect on me. These include many fantastic trainers such as Grant Cardone, Sam Bryant, Dave Anderson, David Kain, Jackie Cooper, Joe Verde, Jeff Sacks, and Tony Noland. Also included are many authors such as Rush Limbaugh, Bill O'Reilly, Zig Ziglar, Jim Rohn, Frank Bettger, Jim Collins, Pat Riley, Ken Blanchard, Warren Greshes, Dale Carnegie, Newt

Gingrich, and Jeffery Gitomer. In my career, I also had the privilege to work under inspiring leaders such as Patrick O'Brien, Dr. Charles Stanley, B.G. Fuller, Dan Vaden, William Bradshaw, Jerry Richardson, Johnny Love, Michael Love, Walter Lewis, Tony Hill, Michael Offer, and Bill Phillips. Special thanks go to Dave Moon without whose input and collaboration this book would not exist.

In your journey to becoming an exceptional leader, I suggest that you draw from the example of those around you. This includes both those who inspire you, those who are members of your team, those on whose team you support, and your family. Learn your craft, lead boldly, and take <u>massive action</u> to achieve your goals. Your team and your family deserve no less than your very best!

And remember . . .

**"Education without Action
is just Entertainment!"**

ADDITIONAL READING LIST

Dave Anderson
It is Not Rocket Science: 4 Simple Strategies for Mastering the Art of Execution
No-Nonsense Leadership

Zig Ziglar
Top Performance: How to Develop Excellence in Yourself and Others
See You at the Top
Secrets of Closing the Sale

Grant Cardone
Sell or be Sold
The 10X Rule

Dale Carnegie
How to Win Friends and Influence People
How to Stop Working and Start Living

Jim Collins
Good to Great
Built to Last

Pat Riley
The Winner Within

Joe Verde
Growth: High Achievers vs. Amateurs

Frank Bettger
How I Raised Myself from Failure to Success through Selling

Jim Rohn
The Power of Ambition, Unleashing the Conquering Drive within You

Warren Greshes
Supercharged Goal Setting
Supercharged Selling

Ken Blanchard
Leadership and the One Minute Manager
Servant Leader

Jeffery Gitomer
Customer Satisfaction is Worthless: Customer Loyalty is Priceless
The Little Red Book of Selling

RECOMMENDATIONS FOR LARRY A. BONORATO

Jed Fraser: Finance Director

I worked with Larry a number of years at Bradshaw Automotive when he was the General Manager there. Larry is the epitome of professionalism and always believes in inclusiveness. He is a natural leader. I still incorporate much of what I learned from him in my daily activities to this day. His philosophy of sales is both intuitive and disciplined. He believes in bringing a team together and encourages teamwork. I would highly recommend Larry to anyone who is either looking to work with or hire him. There are a lot of talented individuals in the automobile industry, and Larry is in the top 5%.

Grover Fitzgerald; Internet Manager/BDC Director at Vic Bailey Ford

In my more than 17 years in the automotive industry, I can truly say that Larry Bonorato rates as the best General Manager that I have had the pleasure to work with over my time with Saturn. He is detail-oriented, fair, and strives to get the best from those around him. Truly one of the best in the automotive retail industry and is always reaching for the top.

Dave Moon: President at Moon Marketing & Advertising, Inc.

Larry is one of the best managers and team builders I have ever worked with. He is a great motivator and communicator and never seems to run out of positive energy and creative ideas. I would highly recommend Larry as a person of incredible character and ethics and look forward to working with him on any upcoming projects

Betty Urso; Travel Agent at Linda Long Travel

I worked with Larry at several dealerships under a dealer-owned organization. Larry is very detail-oriented and a good leader. He was a General Manager, Sales Trainer and was well skilled in all areas of the dealership. He is very reliable and honest. I would describe him as a good man to work with day in and day out.

Katie Sullivan; Marketing and Customer Experience Director

Larry was a wonderful manager. He was kind and generous. He provided me with so many opportunities for personal growth and helped shape the sales consultant that I became. I am so grateful for all that he did for me.

Lee Maynor: Agency Owner at Goosehead Insurance Agency

Larry makes things happen. He sinks his teeth into any project, and will not let go. He was a lot of fun to work with, kept me on my toes, and taught me a lot.

Richie Christopher: Owner; Owner, Buddy Branding

Larry is a pleasure to work with. He is always prepared and knows what he wants. He knows how to verbalize his thoughts in a positive way that makes him easy to understand and work with. While working with Larry, I was amazed at his level of professionalism and his integrity. I looked up to him for his wealth of experience and his desire to make everyone around him better.

Michael Hudgens: Recruiter at Teleperformance Group

After 38 years in the automotive business, I can attest that Larry Bonorato is an excellent manager. He has high integrity and is one of the best car men I know. He would be an invaluable asset to any company.

John Avery: Kia Digital Consultant at Shift Digital

I worked with Larry for several years with the Bradshaw Auto Group. I have never worked with someone so enthusiastic about what he did. Larry always had a positive attitude and was always looking for ways to better the group and his employees.

LARRY ON LEARNING
Education without Action is Just Entertainment